TAMERLANE

TAMERLANE

Dennis Wepman

1987
CHELSEA HOUSE PUBLISHERS
NEW YORK
NEW HAVEN   PHILADELPHIA

EDITORIAL DIRECTOR: Nancy Toff
MANAGING EDITOR: Karyn Gullen Browne
COPY CHIEF: Perry Scott King
ART DIRECTOR: Giannella Garrett
ASSISTANT ART DIRECTOR: Carol McDougall
PICTURE EDITOR: Elizabeth Terhune

Staff for TAMERLANE:

SENIOR EDITOR: John W. Selfridge
TEXT EDITOR: Marian W. Taylor
ASSISTANT EDITORS: Maria Behan, Pierre Hauser, Howard Ratner, Bert Yaeger
COPY EDITORS: Sean Dolan, Kathleen McDermott
ASSISTANT DESIGNER: Noreen Lamb
PICTURE RESEARCH: Karen Herman
LAYOUT: Irene Friedman
PRODUCTION COORDINATOR: Alma Rodriguez
PRODUCTION ASSISTANT: Karen Dreste
COVER ILLUSTRATION: Laura McDougall

CREATIVE DIRECTOR: Harold Steinberg

Frontispiece courtesy of The Bettmann Archive

First Printing

Library of Congress Cataloging in Publication Data

Wepman, Dennis. TAMERLANE

(World leaders past & present)
Bibliography: p.
Includes index.
1. Timur, 1336–1405—Biography—Juvenile literature.
2. Asia, Central—Kings and rulers—Biography—Juvenile
literature. 3. Conquerors—Asia, Central—Biography—
Juvenile literature. [1. Tamerlane, 1336–1405.
2. Kings, queens, rulers, etc.] I. Title. II. Series.
DS23.W46   1987   950'.2'0924 [B] [92]   86-26334

ISBN 0-87754-442-5

Contents

ADENAUER	FREDERICK THE GREAT	MARY, QUEEN OF SCOTS
ALEXANDER THE GREAT	INDIRA GANDHI	GOLDA MEIR
MARC ANTONY	MOHANDAS GANDHI	METTERNICH
KING ARTHUR	GARIBALDI	MUSSOLINI
ATATÜRK	GENGHIS KHAN	NAPOLEON
ATTLEE	GLADSTONE	NASSER
BEGIN	GORBACHEV	NEHRU
BEN-GURION	HAMMARSKJÖLD	NERO
BISMARCK	HENRY VIII	NICHOLAS II
LÉON BLUM	HENRY OF NAVARRE	NIXON
BOLÍVAR	HINDENBURG	NKRUMAH
CESARE BORGIA	HITLER	PERICLES
BRANDT	HO CHI MINH	PERÓN
BREZHNEV	HUSSEIN	QADDAFI
CAESAR	IVAN THE TERRIBLE	ROBESPIERRE
CALVIN	ANDREW JACKSON	ELEANOR ROOSEVELT
CASTRO	JEFFERSON	FRANKLIN D. ROOSEVELT
CATHERINE THE GREAT	JOAN OF ARC	THEODORE ROOSEVELT
CHARLEMAGNE	POPE JOHN XXIII	SADAT
CHIANG KAI-SHEK	LYNDON JOHNSON	STALIN
CHURCHILL	JUÁREZ	SUN YAT-SEN
CLEMENCEAU	JOHN F. KENNEDY	TAMERLANE
CLEOPATRA	KENYATTA	THATCHER
CORTÉS	KHOMEINI	TITO
CROMWELL	KHRUSHCHEV	TROTSKY
DANTON	MARTIN LUTHER KING, JR.	TRUDEAU
DE GAULLE	KISSINGER	TRUMAN
DE VALERA	LENIN	VICTORIA
DISRAELI	LINCOLN	WASHINGTON
EISENHOWER	LLOYD GEORGE	WEIZMANN
ELEANOR OF AQUITAINE	LOUIS XIV	WOODROW WILSON
QUEEN ELIZABETH I	LUTHER	XERXES
FERDINAND AND ISABELLA	JUDAS MACCABEUS	ZHOU ENLAI
FRANCO	MAO ZEDONG	

ON LEADERSHIP
Arthur M. Schlesinger, jr.

LEADERSHIP, it may be said, is really what makes the world go round. Love no doubt smooths the passage; but love is a private transaction between consenting adults. Leadership is a public transaction with history. The idea of leadership affirms the capacity of individuals to move, inspire, and mobilize masses of people so that they act together in pursuit of an end. Sometimes leadership serves good purposes, sometimes bad; but whether the end is benign or evil, great leaders are those men and women who leave their personal stamp on history.

Now, the very concept of leadership implies the proposition that individuals can make a difference. This proposition has never been universally accepted. From classical times to the present day, eminent thinkers have regarded individuals as no more than the agents and pawns of larger forces, whether the gods and goddesses of the ancient world or, in the modern era, race, class, nation, the dialectic, the will of the people, the spirit of the times, history itself. Against such forces, the individual dwindles into insignificance.

So contends the thesis of historical determinism. Tolstoy's great novel *War and Peace* offers a famous statement of the case. Why, Tolstoy asked, did millions of men in the Napoleonic wars, denying their human feelings and their common sense, move back and forth across Europe slaughtering their fellows? "The war," Tolstoy answered, "was bound to happen simply because it was bound to happen." All prior history predetermined it. As for leaders, they, Tolstoy said, "are but the labels that serve to give a name to an end and, like labels, they have the least possible connection with the event." The greater the leader, "the more conspicuous the inevitability and the predestination of every act he commits." The leader, said Tolstoy, is "the slave of history."

Determinism takes many forms. Marxism is the determinism of class. Nazism the determinism of race. But the idea of men and women as the slaves of history runs athwart the deepest human instincts. Rigid determinism abolishes the idea of human freedom—

the assumption of free choice that underlies every move we make, every word we speak, every thought we think. It abolishes the idea of human responsibility, since it is manifestly unfair to reward or punish people for actions that are by definition beyond their control. No one can live consistently by any deterministic creed. The Marxist states prove this themselves by their extreme susceptibility to the cult of leadership.

More than that, history refutes the idea that individuals make no difference. In December 1931 a British politician crossing Park Avenue in New York City between 76th and 77th Streets around 10:30 P.M. looked in the wrong direction and was knocked down by an automobile—a moment, he later recalled, of a man aghast, a world aglare: "I do not understand why I was not broken like an eggshell or squashed like a gooseberry." Fourteen months later an American politician, sitting in an open car in Miami, Florida, was fired on by an assassin; the man beside him was hit. Those who believe that individuals make no difference to history might well ponder whether the next two decades would have been the same had Mario Constasino's car killed Winston Churchill in 1931 and Giuseppe Zangara's bullet killed Franklin Roosevelt in 1933. Suppose, in addition, that Adolf Hitler had been killed in the street fighting during the Munich *Putsch* of 1923 and that Lenin had died of typhus during World War I. What would the 20th century be like now?

For better or for worse, individuals do make a difference. "The notion that a people can run itself and its affairs anonymously," wrote the philosopher William James, "is now well known to be the silliest of absurdities. Mankind does nothing save through initiatives on the part of inventors, great or small, and imitation by the rest of us—these are the sole factors in human progress. Individuals of genius show the way, and set the patterns, which common people then adopt and follow."

Leadership, James suggests, means leadership in thought as well as in action. In the long run, leaders in thought may well make the greater difference to the world. But, as Woodrow Wilson once said, "Those only are leaders of men, in the general eye, who lead in action. . . . It is at their hands that new thought gets its translation into the crude language of deeds." Leaders in thought often invent in solitude and obscurity, leaving to later generations the tasks of imitation. Leaders in action—the leaders portrayed in this series—have to be effective in their own time.

And they cannot be effective by themselves. They must act in response to the rhythms of their age. Their genius must be adapted, in a phrase of William James's, "to the receptivities of the moment." Leaders are useless without followers. "There goes the mob," said the French politician hearing a clamor in the streets. "I am their leader. I must follow them." Great leaders turn the inchoate emotions of the mob to purposes of their own. They seize on the opportunities of their time, the hopes, fears, frustrations, crises, potentialities. They succeed when events have prepared the way for them, when the community is awaiting to be aroused, when they can provide the clarifying and organizing ideas. Leadership ignites the circuit between the individual and the mass and thereby alters history.

It may alter history for better or for worse. Leaders have been responsible for the most extravagant follies and most monstrous crimes that have beset suffering humanity. They have also been vital in such gains as humanity has made in individual freedom, religious and racial tolerance, social justice and respect for human rights.

There is no sure way to tell in advance who is going to lead for good and who for evil. But a glance at the gallery of men and women in *World Leaders—Past and Present* suggests some useful tests.

One test is this: do leaders lead by force or by persuasion? By command or by consent? Through most of history leadership was exercised by the divine right of authority. The duty of followers was to defer and to obey. "Theirs not to reason why,/ Theirs but to do and die." On occasion, as with the so-called "enlightened despots" of the 18th century in Europe, absolutist leadership was animated by humane purposes. More often, absolutism nourished the passion for domination, land, gold and conquest and resulted in tyranny.

The great revolution of modern times has been the revolution of equality. The idea that all people should be equal in their legal condition has undermined the old structure of authority, hierarchy and deference. The revolution of equality has had two contrary effects on the nature of leadership. For equality, as Alexis de Tocqueville pointed out in his great study *Democracy in America*, might mean equality in servitude as well as equality in freedom.

"I know of only two methods of establishing equality in the political world," Tocqueville wrote. "Rights must be given to every citizen, or none at all to anyone . . . save one, who is the master of all." There was no middle ground "between the sovereignty of all and the absolute power of one man." In his astonishing prediction of 20th-century totalitarian dictatorship, Tocqueville explained how the revolution of equality could lead to the *"Führerprinzip"* and more terrible absolutism than the world had ever known.

But when rights are given to every citizen and the sovereignty of all is established, the problem of leadership takes a new form, becomes more exacting than ever before. It is easy to issue commands and enforce them by the rope and the stake, the concentration camp and the *gulag.* It is much harder to use argument and achievement to overcome opposition and win consent. The Founding Fathers of the United States understood the difficulty. They believed that history had given them the opportunity to decide, as Alexander Hamilton wrote in the first Federalist Paper, whether men are indeed capable of basing government on "reflection and choice, or whether they are forever destined to depend . . . on accident and force."

Government by reflection and choice called for a new style of leadership and a new quality of followership. It required leaders to be responsive to popular concerns, and it required followers to be active and informed participants in the process. Democracy does not eliminate emotion from politics; sometimes it fosters demagoguery; but it is confident that, as the greatest of democratic leaders put it, you cannot fool all of the people all of the time. It measures leadership by results and retires those who overreach or falter or fail.

It is true that in the long run despots are measured by results too. But they can postpone the day of judgment, sometimes indefinitely, and in the meantime they can do infinite harm. It is also true that democracy is no guarantee of virtue and intelligence in government, for the voice of the people is not necessarily the voice of God. But democracy, by assuring the right of opposition, offers built-in resistance to the evils inherent in absolutism. As the theologian Reinhold Niebuhr summed it up, "Man's capacity for justice makes democracy possible, but man's inclination to injustice makes democracy necessary."

A second test for leadership is the end for which power is sought. When leaders have as their goal the supremacy of a master race or the promotion of totalitarian revolution or the acquisition and exploitation of colonies or the protection of greed and privilege or the preservation of personal power, it is likely that their leadership will do little to advance the cause of humanity. When their goal is the abolition of slavery, the liberation of women, the enlargement of opportunity for the poor and powerless, the extension of equal rights to racial minorities, the defense of the freedoms of expression and opposition, it is likely that their leadership will increase the sum of human liberty and welfare.

Leaders have done great harm to the world. They have also conferred great benefits. You will find both sorts in this series. Even "good" leaders must be regarded with a certain wariness. Leaders are not demigods; they put on their trousers one leg after another just like ordinary mortals. No leader is infallible, and every leader needs to be reminded of this at regular intervals. Irreverence irritates leaders but is their salvation. Unquestioning submission corrupts leaders and demands followers. Making a cult of a leader is always a mistake. Fortunately hero worship generates its own antidote. "Every hero," said Emerson, "becomes a bore at last."

The signal benefit the great leaders confer is to embolden the rest of us to live according to our own best selves, to be active, insistent, and resolute in affirming our own sense of things. For great leaders attest to the reality of human freedom against the supposed inevitabilities of history. And they attest to the wisdom and power that may lie within the most unlikely of us, which is why Abraham Lincoln remains the supreme example of great leadership. A great leader, said Emerson, exhibits new possibilities to all humanity. "We feed on genius. . . . Great men exist that there may be greater men."

Great leaders, in short, justify themselves by emancipating and empowering their followers. So humanity struggles to master its destiny, remembering with Alexis de Tocqueville: "It is true that around every man a fatal circle is traced beyond which he cannot pass; but within the wide verge of that circle he is powerful and free; as it is with man, so with communities."

—*New York*

1

Chess Player

Tamerlane had been supreme master of his people for almost 30 years, and he was not used to having his orders questioned. Now he had decided to invade India, and his generals were telling him it couldn't be done! They said it would be impossible to move an army from central Asia to India and that even if they got there, their men would be vastly outnumbered by the Indians.

Furthermore, argued the generals, the Indian armies were equipped with a terrifying weapon — huge, savage war elephants. It was said that these beasts could not be hurt by swords or arrows, that they could uproot great trees simply by breathing on them, that they could easily hurl horses and their riders to their deaths.

Tamerlane was the most powerful man of his time, an Oriental ruler who held more land and ruled more people than anyone else in the world. Wherever he led his army, he triumphed. His empire already stretched from central Asia to Turkey, from southern Russia to India's northern border. It included most of present-day Iran, Iraq, Turkey, Syria, and Afghanistan. Now, in the year 1398, the 62-

> *All Asia is in arms with Tamburlaine. . . . The scourge of God and terror of the world.*
> —CHRISTOPHER MARLOWE
> 16th-century dramatist,
> from *Tamburlaine the Great*

This likeness of Tamerlane (1336–1405) was modeled from his skull, revealed when his tomb in Samarkand (now part of the Soviet Union) was opened in 1941. The skeleton in the tomb, reported archeologists, was that of a crippled but extraordinarily powerful man. He had been 5 feet, 7 inches tall.

Pisces (the fish) and Gemini (the twins) appear in an astrological manuscript written shortly before Tamerlane's time. The Mongol leader (whose own sign was Aries, the ram) always consulted his court astrologer before he engaged in battle.

year-old Tamerlane was determined to add India to his conquests.

Tamerlane and his people were Mongols, members of a racial division whose physical appearance is marked by yellowish skin, high, prominent cheekbones, straight black hair, and broad faces. Mongolian people are also distinguished by their eyes, which are shielded by a fold of skin above the eyelid. Mongols were—and still are—native to central Asia.

The Mongol leader was taller than most of his contemporaries. He had a lame right leg and stiff right arm — reputedly the results of a youthful sheep-stealing raid — but his lameness did nothing to diminish his awesome strength in combat or his air of complete self-assurance. His commanding presence was underscored by his proud, erect posture. Few men dared to stand up to this imposing chieftain.

Tamerlane's real name was Timur (pronounced Tim-OOR), which in the Mongol and Turkish languages means "iron." The Persians, who hated him, called him Timur-leng, or "Timur the Lame." The contemptuous nickname stuck, and his name has come into Western history as Tamerlane. In 1587 English playwright Christopher Marlowe wrote *Tamburlaine the Great*, a powerful poetic drama that is still performed. Marlowe called Tamerlane "the scourge of God and terror of the world."

The Mongol chief knew what he wanted, and he knew how to get it. He knew that India had been weakened by the 10 years of chaos and civil war that had followed the death of its king, Firoz-Shah. He knew that India was ripe for conquest. He knew that Allah (the Muslim name for God) would favor his conquest of India's Hindu "idol worshipers." Dismissing the protests of his advisers, he mobilized his forces and headed south.

Tamerlane divided his army into three parts. He sent one section into the Indian area known as the Punjab and another against the Indian city of Lahore. Choosing—as always—the hardest, most dangerous route for himself, he led the third arm of the invasion force through the forbidding Hindu Kush mountain range.

Fortune, my children, furnishes us with such happy opportunities, that it appears as if she offered herself to us, and called upon us to profit by them. For, as we have already seen . . . almost all Asia under our command, she now shows us India, through the disorders of the princes who govern her, opening her gates to receive us.
—TAMERLANE
to his council of amirs
in 1398

The Indians ferociously resisted Tamerlane's invading army. Accustomed to the bitter mountain weather and the treacherous terrain, they were able to inflict heavy casualties on the invaders. Time after time they lured the Mongol army up icy peaks and then vanished into the swirling snows, leaving their enemies stranded and bewildered. Tamerlane and his soldiers often had to slide down on improvised toboggans and lower their horses on slings. Many disappeared over the edges of cliffs into the trackless snow below.

At last the haggard survivors of the long march through the mountains reached the Indus River, crossed it, and began what has been called "one of the cruelest and maddest campaigns . . . known to the history of Asia."

Tamerlane's troops were merciless. They fell on India's proud old cities and, one by one, picked them clean and destroyed them. Word of the invaders' implacable fury spread. When the fortress city of Bhatnir refused to open its gates to the invaders, Tamerlane ordered his men to storm the walls. Rather than fall into the hands of the Mongols, the city's terrified residents set their own houses on fire and threw themselves and their families into the raging flames.

Wherever they went, Tamerlane's men looted and killed. In every city and town, they slaughtered the children and seized the healthy adults as slaves. By the time the Mongols reached the ancient and wealthy Indian city of Delhi, their baggage trains — filled with gold and ivory, gems and fabrics, cattle and slaves—were immense.

Delhi had been the cultural and political center of India's rich civilization for centuries. Its rulers and most of its citizens were, like Tamerlane and his people, Muslims.

Tamerlane's wars were waged for loot and slaves. He was in the habit, however, of justifying them as wars against the enemies of Islam, the Muslim faith. Tamerlane was careful to note that despite Delhi's Muslim traditions, its rulers had been lax with infidels; the city was, therefore, an obvious target for his conquest.

A 14th-century Indian artist painted Tamerlane (center)
in traditional Mongol battle dress: pointed helmet and
armor covered by a kuyuk, a sleeveless velvet jacket.

A modern highway now covers the route — known as the "Road of Thirst" — along which Tamerlane and his army marched to India in 1398. The Mongols' path led them through the grim and towering Hindu Kush mountains, some of them reaching the height of 25,000 feet.

Delhi's sultan sat confidently on his high throne, his rule backed by his highly trained army and his famed war elephants. Dressed for battle, these animals were like primitive tanks. They wore heavy armor and, at the ends of their tusks, sharp swords. On their backs were platforms from which Indian soldiers could hurl lances and fire crossbows.

Tamerlane feared that his army's Indian captives would stage a revolt during the battle for Delhi, so he ordered his men to put their prisoners to death at once. It is said that at Tamerlane's command his soldiers strangled 100,000 Indian slaves at the gates of Delhi in less than an hour. Then the Mongol chief consulted his astrologers and, with his troops, lay flat on the ground to ask Allah's aid in their battle against the Indians. His preparations completed, he set forth to take the fabled city.

Concealing most of his men, Tamerlane ordered a small detachment of soldiers to camp outside the walls. He told this group to scurry about in seeming confusion, giving the appearance of fear and disorder. Tamerlane believed that this performance would make the sultan feel secure enough to send his army out to attack. He was right. The attack was ordered, and the fate of Delhi was sealed.

The few confused soldiers the sultan had seen from his high towers in Delhi suddenly turned into 90,000 horsemen, disciplined to act as one. The Indian elephants trumpeted and charged, but Tamerlane had planted their path with barbed stakes and armed his troops with devices that hurled pots of burning pitch. Injured and panicky, the mighty beasts stampeded, crushing to death many of the Indian soldiers. The Indians defended their city furiously, but they were overwhelmed by the Mongol army, which forced them back to the gates of the city. Realizing the battle had been lost, the sultan fled, and the splendid city of Delhi fell to Tamerlane and his men.

At first, Tamerlane spared the lives of Delhi's inhabitants, contenting himself with the payment of huge ransoms. He settled down to enjoy his victory, holding lavish feasts and reviewing the surviving war elephants, now his property. "These well-

This relatively cultured man, a lover of Persian literature and Iranian art, in making contact with one of the most polished civilizations of the Old World behaved like the leader of a horde, plundering for the sake of plunder, massacring and destroying through blindness or closed-mindedness to a certain set of cultural values.
—RENÉ GROUSSET
French historian,
on Tamerlane's invasion of India

A pair of huge stone elephants guard one of the seven gates leading into the Indian city of Delhi. Tamerlane destroyed the ancient capital city in 1398; modern "Old Delhi," surrounded by a 30-foot-high wall, was built almost two centuries later.

This Indian servant, like
thousands of others em-
ployed by the ruling Muslims
of 14th-century Delhi, was a
Hindu. Tamerlane and his
men were Muslims, but when
they laid siege to Delhi, they
showed no more mercy to
their fellow Muslims in the
city than they did to the "in-
fidel" Hindus.

THE BETTMANN ARCHIVE

trained elephants," according to a contemporary writer, "bowed their heads and knelt before him in obeisance, and all trumpeted at the same time, as if rendering homage."

The Mongols' peaceful occupation of the city was not to last long. When Delhi's residents began to protest the demands made on them by the invaders, Tamerlane's men reacted with fury. They massacred everyone except the people they wanted as slaves; as a chronicler of the time put it, "The soldiers hurried to pounce on the population like hungry wolves falling on a flock of sheep." The Mongols seized everything they could carry and burned the rest. Even Tamerlane was said to be appalled by his men's savagery. He tried to calm them, but there was no stemming the storm of greed and fury.

In a few days Delhi was destroyed completely. Shadowing each of the city's four corners was a tower of human heads. The few Indians who managed to escape the carnage soon died of hunger or disease. "For two whole months," reported one witness, "not a bird moved a wing in the city." A century and a half would pass before the stately city of Delhi was rebuilt.

Every soldier in Tamerlane's ranks came home rich. Some took coins or precious stones; some took rare ivories or gold plates; all took slaves. The high lords, who had first choice, each picked about 100 men and women. It was reported that "when Timur returned . . . there were none of his followers who did not have at least 20 slaves abducted from India."

Tamerlane was heir to a tradition of fierceness and ruthlessness. His ancestors, worshipers of the sky god Tengri, had seen their conquests as necessary; they had allowed nothing to stand in the way of their god's work.

Although Tamerlane was a Muslim, he had lost none of the single-minded, inflexible dedication of his forefathers. He, too, saw himself as a messenger of God, obliged to destroy those "infidels" who did not worship Allah. He saw the spoils of war as his natural right. But he wanted even more than gold and jewels, elephants and slaves.

Like his men, Tamerlane returned laden with loot.

Tamerlane was tall and lofty of stature . . . mighty in strength and courage, wonderful in nature, white in color, mixed with red, but not dark, stout of limb, with broad shoulders, thick fingers, long legs, perfect build, long beard . . . with eyes like candles, without brilliance; powerful in voice; he did not fear death.
—ACHMED IBN-ARABSHAH
14th-century historian

Ali Baba, hero of a story in *The Arabian Nights' Entertainment*, a 10th-century collection of Persian and Indian folk tales, discovers treasure in a robbers' cave. Even such legendary riches paled in comparison to the loot carried home by Tamerlane's warriors.

But his share of the booty included something different. While the massacre raged about him, the grizzled Mongol chieftain admired the grandeur of the Muslim city, with its towering palaces and thousand-pillared mosque (house of worship) soaring to the sky. When the slaves were selected, he announced a single, special command: All the stonemasons were his.

Tamerlane was something more than a Mongolian bandit who plundered and terrorized a continent. He was also a great builder, a spreader of culture, and, in his way, a man of vision. When he returned to the north to Samarkand, his capital, he brought with him builders and plans for constructing a mosque equal to the one he had pulled down. The ruins of this monument to his soaring aspirations can be seen in Samarkand to this day.

A map of the 14th-century world would have looked very different from a modern one. Europe was not to know of the New World for another century and had only the dimmest ideas about what lay to the east. Huge empires, their cultures far more advanced than Europe's, had risen and fallen in Asia for thousands of years before Tamerlane's time.

Cyrus II, king of Persia in the 6th century B.C., had built a vast and mighty empire that stretched from the Aegean Sea to the Indus River. Two centuries later, Alexander the Great destroyed Cyrus's kingdom and incorporated it into his own. In the 13th and 14th centuries, the great powers in the East were the Mongol khans (rulers) who had swept out of central Asia. When Genghis Khan, the first of these powerful Mongol leaders, died in 1227, his three sons ruled half the known world.

But Genghis's empire was not to last. His sons argued, and their sons fought; conquered provinces rebelled, and ambitious men seized power. By Tamerlane's time, the great Mongol empire was fragmented into a loose confederation of quarreling kingdoms. After Genghis Khan's death, many leaders had dreamed of restoring his awesome domain, but none had succeeded. When Tamerlane determined to march on India in 1398, he sought ter-

> *They say that on the night on which he was born . . . his palms were full of freshly shed blood. They consulted the augurs and referred to seers and soothsayers . . . of whom some replied that he would be a guardsman; others that he would grow up a brigand, while others said a bloodthirsty butcher, others finally that he would be an executioner.*
> —ACHMED IBN-ARABSHAH
> 14th-century historian,
> on the birth of Tamerlane

ritory that even his celebrated predecessor had failed to capture nearly two centuries earlier.

Tamerlane was born on April 9, 1336, near a village in Transoxiana, now part of the southern portion of the Soviet Union. His birthplace was south of Samarkand, which is still an important city in Russia. Sometimes called Tartars or Tatars, Tamerlane's people spoke Turkish and practiced the Muslim religion. In the 14th century there were no national boundaries as there are today. Tamerlane's family belonged to the Barlas clan, one of a group of tribes with ever-shifting loyalties, spread across central Asia.

Takina-Khatun, Tamerlane's mother, died when he was very young. His father, Taraghay, was a minor noble of the Barlas, whose chief was Tamerlane's uncle, Hajji Barlas. When Tamerlane was still a boy, his deeply religious father joined a monastery, leaving his young son quite alone.

Virtually raised in the saddle, the Barlas were superb horsemen. Young Tamerlane was among the best of them, always taking the lead when he rode with his friends. Observers said that although he played with other children, he never laughed and rarely smiled. Those who remembered Tamerlane's youth used the same word to describe him: *serious.*

Little was recorded about Tamerlane's early life, although many legends about it sprang up. One of the most widely believed tales concerned his first appearance: he was said to have been born with his palms filled with blood. "This was understood," ran one account, "to mean that blood would be shed by his hand."

It is known that Tamerlane always loved the game of chess, which he played with great skill. In later life, wanting to further explore the possibilities of the game, he had a special board constructed with twice the usual number of squares and extra pieces. He enjoyed playing chess alone as much as he liked playing the game with others.

While he was still a teenager, Tamerlane built up a following of youths like himself. They admired the sturdy, silent horseman and obeyed his orders unquestioningly. They went with him on his hunting

These fragments of tile, unearthed in modern Samarkand, probably once decorated a mosque or palace of Tamerlane's era. Most of the spectacular buildings in the Mongol chieftain's capital were constructed by craftsmen captured during raids into neighboring territories.

27

Stonemasons and artisans, assisted by elephants, work on the great mosque Tamerlane built in Samarkand when he returned from India. The mosque, Tamerlane's crowning architectural achievement, survived centuries of wars and earthquakes; in the early 1900s it was used to stable the Russian tsar's cavalry horses.

— and thieving — expeditions, sharing the deer and the sheep they brought home. With no laws to violate, men took what they could; everyone had to protect his own property. The band rode free, and Tamerlane called no man his master.

The number of wives a man in Tamerlane's world could have was limited only by his ability to support them. By the time he was 19, Tamerlane already had two wives. Almost nothing is known of them except that each bore her husband a son in 1355. Tamerlane's firstborn was Jahangir, whose name meant "worldgripper"; his second child was Omar-Sheik. Tamerlane was to outlive them both.

When Genghis Khan died in 1227, his kingdom was divided among his descendants. In the northwest, his grandson Batu commanded the people known as the Golden Horde; in the southwest, Genghis's grandson Orda ruled the White Horde; the east was ruled by Genghis's son Chagatai. Over the years Chagatai's descendants quarreled, and his domain was split up. By the middle of the 14th century, the Chagatai kingdom was a small remnant, to the northeast of Transoxiana, of what had been Genghis Khan's empire. Its people were called Jats ("Jat" meant "thief" in the dialect of Transoxiana); they were, like Tamerlane's tribe, Muslims.

Although Genghis's descendants fought among themselves, they never relinquished their dominion. Nomadic peoples like the Barlas lived uncertain lives among the established powers. If an ambitious young man like Tamerlane hoped to rise in life, he had no choice but to leave the green valley of his tribe and enter a wider area, a larger chessboard.

In 1360 Transoxiana was conquered by Tughlugh-Timur, a powerful Jat khan. As the khan advanced into the territory ruled by Tamerlane's uncle, Hajji Barlas, the tribal leader fled. Ever the chess strategist, the 24-year-old Tamerlane now saw his opportunity to emerge from obscurity. Taking his few sheep, goats, horses, and camels — the only possessions his father had given him — he rode away to the court of Tughlugh-Timur.

Tamerlane did not approach the mighty khan as a spokesman for his vanquished tribe. Instead —

> *Tamerlane was of that nomad stock which cultivated the military arts inherited from Genghis Khan, which scorned the settled peasant, and which took fierce pride in the skills of the mounted wanderer.*
> —HILDA HOOKHAM
> British historian

EASTFOTO

Genghis Khan — whose name meant "universal ruler" — was Tamerlane's predecessor as chief of the Mongol people. Like Tamerlane, he was an imaginative leader, a military genius, and a merciless conqueror; his regime was responsible for millions of deaths.

hoping to take his uncle's place as ruler of the Barlas — he offered his services to the conqueror. Tughlugh-Timur was impressed with the young man's bearing and his profession of loyalty. Just as Tamerlane had hoped, the khan placed him in command of his clan and its lands.

As should follow a good opening move in chess, everything went well for a time. Tamerlane took up the governorship of his new territory. He soon formed a close alliance with the ruler of neighboring Balkh, Amir Husayn, who controlled the region now known as Afghanistan. Tamerlane earned Husayn's gratitude by helping his neighbor put down several rebellions in his own area. The relationship between the two men was strengthened when Tamerlane took Husayn's sister, Uljay-Turkan-Agha, as one of his wives.

Soon after Tamerlane's rise to power, Hajji Barlas

reappeared on the scene. Apparently not as shrewd as his nephew, Hajji spoke out against the khan; soon afterward, he was assassinated. Following the ancient laws of revenge, Tamerlane hunted down his uncle's killers and put them to death with his own hands.

Despite his public rage at Hajji's fate, Tamerlane must have been relieved; with his uncle gone, he had no rivals for the leadership of the Barlas. Tughlugh-Timur, expressing strong approval of Tamerlane's leadership, made him adviser to his son, who was viceroy of Transoxiana. It seemed as though Tamerlane's continued success was assured.

Few things in life, however, are certain. Bypassing Tamerlane, Tughlugh-Timur suddenly appointed another man as the highest-ranking administrator in his son's government. Meanwhile, Tamerlane's friend and brother-in-law, Amir Husayn, had rebelled against Tughlugh-Timur; defeated by the khan, Husayn had disappeared into the desert. Tamerlane was alone again, his ambition thwarted, his closest ally gone, his future cloudy. If he had ever needed his skills as a chess player, it was now.

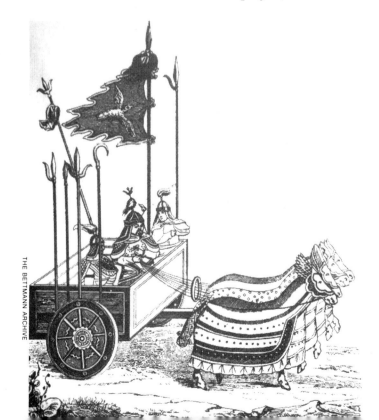

THE BETTMANN ARCHIVE

Chinese soldiers drive a war chariot against the forces of Genghis Khan. The Mongol leader invaded northern China in 1211 and captured its capital, Peking, in 1215. Following in Genghis's footsteps, Tamerlane would attempt an invasion of China in early 1405.

2
Outlaw

Tamerlane was still the "prince of Samarkand" —
the title bestowed on him by Tughlugh-Timur—but,
at least for the moment, his expectations of power
had vanished. Another man held the post of chief
administrator to the khan's son, and that man's
position was safeguarded by one of Tughlugh's generals. This was not what the ambitious young warrior had dreamed of.

Tamerlane did not like being supervised by the
haughty border Mongols who comprised Tughlugh's forces; he liked even less the way the rapa-
cious Jats governed his homeland. Now firmly in
control of Transoxiana, they were looting its cities,
selling its women, and extorting money from the
people. When Tamerlane sent complaints to the
khan, they were ignored.

When he had first presented himself to Tughlugh,
it was not as a defender of the Transoxianian people
but as a willing vassal ready to cooperate with the
Jats. Now he began to see himself in a new light.
As his countrymen groaned under the harsh rule of
the alien troops, Tamerlane saw a great chance for
himself. He could achieve the power he had always

*If heaven be a bow and destiny
the arrow, the marksman is
Allah. Where can you flee
to escape him?*
—ZAIN AD-DIN
Muslim holy man, to
Tamerlane on Tughlugh-
Timur's invasion
of Transoxiana

**Tamerlane was renowned for his upright bearing despite
an early injury that left him with a lame right arm and
leg. His appearance impressed even his enemies, one of
whom described him as "strong and robust in body, brave
and fearless, like a hard rock."**

wanted by freeing his country from the oppression of the outsiders. With his angry people behind him, he would stage a rebellion and regain control of Transoxiana.

Believing he had widespread popular support, Tamerlane mobilized a handful of his most trusted warriors and attacked the khan's forces in Samarkand. The city's residents, however, lost their courage at the last moment; the throngs of armed people Tamerlane had expected to rally to his side never materialized.

Stunned, he led his small band of soldiers into the wasteland. There he overtook messengers carrying orders from the khan to his army in Samarkand. Among the orders was Tamerlane's death warrant. The prince of Samarkand had become a fugitive.

Riding with his few remaining followers across the barren red clay of the plain, Tamerlane was angry and disappointed, but he still believed in his own high destiny. In a short time, he found his brother-in-law Husayn, now a fugitive like himself. Although there were deep differences in temperament and a certain rivalry between the two, they thought it best to pool their slim resources and take their chances together. Their joint forces totaled some 60 men.

The little outlaw band lived like Robin Hood and his men, depending on their wits and courage, always keeping one step ahead of their enemies. Any arguments between Tamerlane and Husayn were controlled by their need to cooperate if they were to survive. They did not always work well together, but both were daring and often brilliant fighters, and they depended on each other.

Their interdependence was demonstrated at Khiva, a city several hundred miles to the northwest of Samarkand. Knowing that the capture of the two famous fugitives would bring a handsome reward from the Jats, the wily lord of the city invited them to stay with him. Tamerlane and Husayn saw the trap and rode off, but the Khivan leader dispatched hundreds of heavily armed horsemen to bring the fugitives back.

Intricate mosaics decorate the entrance of the Shahi-Zinda shrine, still standing in Samarkand. Tamerlane built magnificent tombs for all his family members; this one contained the remains of his female relatives. Among them was Qutluq-Turkan-Agha, the sister who sheltered him while he was a fugitive from Khan Tughlugh-Timur.

Robin Hood, the legendary 12th-century English outlaw, was celebrated for his courage, leadership, and skill with weapons — as was Tamerlane 200 years later. Robin Hood, however, robbed from the rich to help the poor. Tamerlane robbed to serve himself.

Tamerlane, Husayn, and their 60 men fought the attackers with a ferocity born of desperation. Struck with an arrow, Husayn's horse threw him; only Tamerlane's swift action saved Husayn from being hacked to pieces by the Khivans. The battle continued until nightfall, when the beleaguered survivors of the Khivan attack escaped. Only 10 of the original 60 soldiers remained, and of these, 3 soon deserted the fugitives' band. Tamerlane and Husayn decided to separate and meet again, if possible, in Kabul, Husayn's former capital (and Afghanistan's present-day capital). Tamerlane and one of his wives rode off with a single soldier as escort.

The wayfarers spent weeks crossing the desert, depending for food on what little game they could catch. Once they fell into the hands of Ali-Bey, a Persian lord who locked them up in a filthy cow shed. After 62 days, the lord's brother arrived, recognized Tamerlane, and warned Ali-Bey that it might be dangerous to get involved with Transoxianian nobility.

Ali-Bey finally released the prisoners, but he kept their fine horses and other belongings, giving them only a scrawny horse and an ancient camel. The experience of living in the rat-infested shed made a deep impression on the free-riding Tamerlane. He vowed that even though he might kill others in battle or as punishment for crimes, he would never keep anyone in prison.

In 1362 Tamerlane returned to Samarkand, where he spent six weeks hiding in his sister's house. From there he contacted old and trusted friends. He was still a fugitive with a price on his head, but there were always daring men in Samarkand ready to join a desperate enterprise. Gradually, he assembled a small band of followers. When he rejoined Husayn in Kabul, their combined forces numbered 1,000.

With so small an army, Tamerlane and Husayn had no hope of starting a rebellion. That, in fact, was not their object at this point. They were mercenaries, hired fighters like the gunmen of the American West, available to anyone who would pay for their services.

Their first job was in the nearby province of Sistan, in what is now southern Afghanistan. The province's amir (local ruler), Jalal-u-Din, had lost his seven principal garrisons in a recent rebellion, and he offered to pay Tamerlane and Husayn to recover them. The adventurers accepted the assignment and attacked several of the rebel fortresses.

After Tamerlane and Husayn had subdued four of the forts, the commanders of the remaining three surrendered to the amir. They warned him that if Tamerlane took all seven forts he would have control over the whole province, and that once Tamerlane controlled something he was not likely to give it

The deliberateness of his rise to power, with the cold calculation that enabled him to yield when necessary and go into exile when the game required it, is reminiscent of Genghis Khan.
—RENÉ GROUSSET
French historian,
on Tamerlane

The ancient city of Khiva was the scene of a close call for Tamerlane and his brother-in-law Husayn. Hoping to collect a reward from the Jats, the city's lord tried to trap the pair; they escaped, but the effort cost them 50 of their 60 men.

up. Seeing the logic of this argument, Jalal-u-Din joined the rebel side and attacked Tamerlane and Husayn himself.

The mercenary fighters gave a good account of themselves, quickly defeating the combined forces of the amir and the rebels. As a business venture, however, the action was less than satisfactory, since the amir was obviously no longer interested in paying them for their work. Undaunted, Tamerlane and Husayn paid themselves with plunder. Their success caused their reputation to grow, and as their fame increased, so did the number of their forces.

The fighting force they assembled began to attract the support of the unhappy amirs under Tughlugh-Timur's rule. The outlaw band began staging raids on border detachments of Tughlugh's soldiers. Their first decisive victory was at Tamerlane's home city of Shahrisabz — known as the Green City — where he knew he would find supporters. Since he was heavily outnumbered, he had to depend on cunning, which was always one of his strongest qualities. Commenting on Tamerlane's military style, a contemporary biographer said, "Weigh not lightly any act or trick of a foe; for sometimes the fox has overthrown lions."

The trick Tamerlane employed in his attack on the Green City was an old one among desert fighters, but the soldiers of the Jat garrison were not familiar with it. As he approached the city, he ordered his men to cut branches from poplar trees and tie them to the sides of their horses. The handful of advancing soldiers stirred up so much dust that the men at the garrison thought a vast army was attacking and ran off without striking a blow. Tamerlane, as a chronicler of the time noted admiringly, had thus "captured a city by dust."

Throwing dust in his enemies' eyes was not the only trick practiced by this desert fox. The major victory of this campaign was accomplished by an even more daring and ingenious ruse, one that has become famous in Asian military history.

In the course of the year 1363, the now numerous outlaws had become extremely troublesome to the viceroy of Transoxiana, Tughlugh's son Ilyas-Khoja.

A showdown was inevitable. When Tamerlane and Husayn crossed the Oxus River, bringing the fighting to the center of his kingdom, Ilyas decided to hurl his entire 20,000-man army against the 6,000 rebels. Tamerlane chose an isolated stone bridge as the place for the battle.

Stationing 2,000 of his best men at the entrance to the bridge, he brought the rest of his army downstream and crossed the river during the night. The Jats were ready to fight, but knowing that 2,000 troops were too few for a serious attack, they feared an ambush and decided to wait until they could find the rest of Tamerlane's men.

All the next day the Jat scouts searched the opposite bank, but they found nothing. That night Tamerlane and Husayn lighted huge bonfires in the hills behind the Jat camp. Believing he was surrounded, Ilyas fled to open ground, exactly what the outlaws wanted him to do. Here, where the Jats were at a great disadvantage, Tamerlane and Husayn attacked in full force.

Scattered and confused, the Jats suffered fearful losses. Ilyas-Khoja himself barely escaped capture. But the Jat troops fought desperately, and their superior numbers took their toll of the enemy. They might have prevailed in the end had not the rebel forces had a singular piece of good luck. As Ilyas withdrew to regroup his troops for a last desperate thrust, he received word that his father, Tughlugh-Timur, had died.

This news changed everything. Winning the battle of the stone bridge was important to Ilyas, but not as important as claiming the crown left by Tughlugh-Timur before a rival came to seize it. With a shout, Ilyas wheeled about and rode off for his home city. Tamerlane and Husayn pursued him, but the new khan of the Jats made his escape.

The war was over. Tamerlane, who had conquered a city by dust, had, in the words of the same chronicler, defeated a great army by campfires. And Transoxiana was free of the Jats.

The two brothers-in-law rode triumphantly into Samarkand as liberators. After a round of celebratory feasts, they set about establishing a new gov-

> *Accurst be he that first invented war.*
> —CHRISTOPHER MARLOWE
> 16th-century dramatist,
> from *Tamburlaine the Great*

Kabul, capital of modern Afghanistan, was once the capital of Balkh, the land ruled by Amir Husayn.

ernment — a move that triggered new trouble. The uncertain bond that had held Tamerlane and Husayn together in time of peril quickly frayed in this period of peace. Each now sought the support of his own followers, and every lord in the kingdom fought to protect his own independence and influence.

At last a council of nobles was called, and the assembled amirs decided to give the throne of Transoxiana to a member of the Chagatai family, a direct descendant of Genghis Khan. The new khan was to be ruler in name only; both Husayn and Tamerlane expected to be the real powers behind the throne.

A sufficiently weak and unambitious royal descendant was found in Kabul-Shah, a poet and religious ascetic who drank no wine, never touched a sword, and spent his days in prayer and fasting. Kabul was crowned and then forgotten.

Meanwhile, Ilyas-Khoja, who had never wholly accepted his defeat at the battle of the stone bridge, was making plans to reclaim Transoxiana. Early in 1365 he mobilized a large force to attack. Tamerlane and Husayn were ready for him; two years of peace had restored their spirits and enabled them to reequip their army. Their mesh armor and steel helmets flashing in the sun, they rode out to meet the Jat army on a riverbank near the city of Tashkent, northeast of Samarkand.

The Transoxianians, for once outnumbering their adversaries, were confident of victory. Suddenly, however, a violent storm broke out. Lightning etched the sky, rain fell in sheets, and in moments the battlefield was deep in mud. The terrified horses thrashed about in the mire and threw their riders, and the river, already high with the melting snows of spring, overflowed.

Worst of all was the thunder, which always frightened the Mongols. A traveler to their region at that period described their reaction to it: "They put all strangers out of their houses," he wrote, "wrapped themselves up in black felt and lay hidden until the thunder was over." At last, with both sides in fear and chaos, the battle ended for the day.

The next day the two armies began again, but the field was still deep in mud, and both sides fared badly. The battle remained about equal for hours, but finally Tamerlane saw a chance to strike directly at the hesitating Ilyas-Khoja. Calling to Husayn for support, he plunged forward. But Husayn, always more cautious than Tamerlane, had all he could do to maintain his own position and refused. That opportunity lost, the Transoxianian army lost the battle and had to retreat, leaving more than 10,000 of their men dead in the mud.

The "Battle of the Mire" cost the Transoxianians more than men; it opened the road to Samarkand. Ilyas, flushed with victory, headed for the great city

Mobility and surprise were his major weapons of attack, but this chess-playing nomad knew when to hold back and how to wait.
—HILDA HOOKHAM
British historian,
on Tamerlane

at once. Having defeated Tamerlane and Husayn, he anticipated no trouble with Samarkand's peaceful merchants and tradesmen. He was, however, in for a surprise. The courageous civilians of Samarkand held the Jats off for weeks, resisting their siege with a tenacity that the battle-weary Jats were unable to break.

The city's defenders, short of food and supplies, were beginning to weaken when the invaders were struck by a mysterious epidemic. Ilyas's soldiers sickened and died, and in a short time, three-quarters of his horses — crucial to victory — lay dead before the walls of Samarkand. Believing the epidemic to be the will of Allah, Ilyas led the trembling remnant of his army home. Little more was ever heard about the fearsome Chagatai khan. The next year Ilyas was assassinated, and his people never troubled Transoxiana again.

Left on their own, Samarkand's defenders established their own government, which ran the city for several months. When Tamerlane and Husayn returned — not quite the heroes they had been after the stone bridge battle — they found a cool welcome. In fact, the city had organized itself so well without them that it was inclined to maintain the civilian government it had elected. But the two amirs would have none of that. They quickly regained control of the city and put the elected leaders to death.

Because Husayn was the grandson of a former khan, he claimed the right to rule, a claim that was backed by the council of Transoxianian nobles. Tamerlane, once again a vassal, accepted the role of Husayn's second-in-command.

Husayn had always been known for his greed, and now he outdid himself. As amir he imposed such heavy taxes that the people groaned as loudly as they had under the harsh regime of the Jats. Hoping to reduce Tamerlane's strength, Husayn demanded especially high payments from his brother-in-law's supporters, many of whom were unable to meet the amir's demands.

Tamerlane, who always spent freely, sold his own possessions to help his friends pay their taxes. At one point he was so hard-pressed that he had to

THE METROPOLITAN MUSEUM OF ART, BEQUEST OF MONROE C. GUTMAN, 1974

Tamerlane's 1363 "campfire victory" against Ilyas-Khoja became the subject of painting, story, and song. Believing himself surrounded when Tamerlane encircled his camp with huge bonfires, Ilyas-Khoja brought his forces into the open, exactly where the wily Mongol leader wanted him.

THE METROPOLITAN MUSEUM OF ART, PURCHASE, FLETCHER FUND AND MARGARET MUSHEKIAN AND MR. AND MRS. JEROME A. STRAKA GIFTS, 1975

A primitive but explicit view of war was offered by a 14th-century artist, who crowded his canvas with severed heads and limbs. Tamerlane's warriors were richly rewarded for their services — if they managed to survive. Battlefield casualty rates were staggering.

send jewelry belonging to his wife Uljay-Turkan as payment. Historians of the time noted that Husayn recognized his sister's earrings but avariciously accepted them anyway.

In 1366 Uljay-Turkan died suddenly; her death snapped the only remaining link between Husayn and Tamerlane. Now the two were merely rivals, and their relationship became even more strained. Tamerlane continued to serve as Husayn's military aide, fighting for him when necessary, but he never really accepted his subordinate role, and he never forgave Husayn for his lack of support during the Battle of the Mire.

The two men finally parted company completely. Tamerlane returned to the life of a free-lance warrior, at one point even offering to join the Jats in attacking Transoxiana. The invasion never occurred, but it was clear that Tamerlane and Husayn would never be allies again.

During the next four years, rivalry and resent-

Muslim pilgrims make their way across the desert to Mecca, Islam's holiest city. Located in present-day Saudi Arabia, Mecca is the place of birth of Islam's founder, the prophet Muhammad (570–632). Center of the Islamic religion, the city has been the destination of Muslim pilgrims for more than 13 centuries.

ment turned into open war, and Tamerlane continually raided Husayn's cities and settlements. Perhaps his most famous campaign during this period was his siege of the large, well-fortified city of Karshi in 1369. With 240 men, Tamerlane staged an attack on the Oxus River city, then crossed the river to make the enemy think he had abandoned the siege. Waiting until his spies told him that Husayn's celebrating men were drunk, he recrossed the river, climbed the city's high walls, and killed the guards. He ordered his men to sound trumpets and rattle drums all around the city to convince the people that they were surrounded by a large force. Most fled. The rest, stupefied by wine or surprise, were cut down where they stood.

Reports of Tamerlane's victory at Karshi brought him new allies. Among those who already supported him were nomadic princes who resented Husayn's anchoring his regime in the region's citadels; city dwellers whose lives were kept off balance by Husayn's incessant wars; ordinary citizens crushed by Husayn's merciless taxes; and people with individual grievances against the amir, one of whom was a warrior named Kay-Khusrau. In 1360 Husayn had killed Kay-Khusrau's brother and appropriated his lands, and Kay-Khusrau had sworn to take revenge on the amir.

When two neighboring amirs joined Tamerlane with 7,000 soldiers, the balance tipped in his favor. He hounded Husayn southward, finally trapping him in the walled fortress city of Balkh, in 1370. Tamerlane's men surrounded the city and, after a fierce battle, broke through its walls and conquered its defenders. One of the heroes of the day was Tamerlane's 16-year-old son; Omar-Sheik, it was written, "gave proof of his valor" during the battle.

Husayn finally offered to surrender on condition that his life be spared. He said that if he was allowed to live, he would give up all his titles and property and leave at once for the holy city of Mecca. According to one version of the story, after Tamerlane had consented to this pathetic plea, Husayn tried to escape. When he was captured, Kay-Khusrau, whose brother Husayn had killed, demanded his right to take revenge. Respecting ancient tradition, Tamerlane gave his consent.

"The Book of Fate already contained the hour and place of Husayn's death," Tamerlane's chronicler offers by way of justification, "and no man can escape his destiny." In the unending violence generated by the custom of seeking "an eye for an eye," Kay-Khusrau was himself later slaughtered by several of Husayn's friends.

Tamerlane now held supreme power in Transoxiana. At the age of 33, he had achieved what might earlier have been his highest ambition. For Tamerlane, however, it was only the first step of a journey that would lead him to one of the most powerful positions on earth.

Like much of the reading material available in Tamerlane's world, this astrological treatise was written in Arabic. Tamerlane never learned to read or write, but he employed scholars fluent in Arabic, Greek, Hebrew, and other languages; with their help, he became well versed in many subjects, including history, astrology, and poetry.

Tamerlan

3

"Lord of the Fortunate Conjunction"

Tamerlane's victory over Husayn made him first of all the lords of central Asia. A contemporary historian reported that on April 10, 1370, Tamerlane "ascended the throne, placed the crown of gold upon his head, and girded himself with the imperial belt in the presence of the princes and amirs, who fell upon their knees."

The nobles who attended the ceremony showered the new lord with jewels and gold, and they addressed him by several titles: Emperor of the Age, Conqueror of the World, and Lord of the Fortunate Conjunction. The last title referred to the planets at the time of his birth; their position was held to be highly favorable to Tamerlane's success.

After Husayn's death, Tamerlane, following the custom of his people, took four of Husayn's wives into his own harem. One of them, Saray-Mulik-Khanum, was the daughter of a former khan. Through his marriage to her, Tamerlane acquired the honorary title *gurgan* — son-in-law — of the khan. The one appellation Tamerlane did not receive was khan. He never pretended to be of the

The advent of Tamerlane was no freak occurrence. His achievements were not fortuitous. He was the most able child of his period.
—HILDA HOOKHAM
British historian

Persian and Indian paintings of Tamerlane are formalized, usually making him look more like an Eastern sultan than a Mongol warrior. No Tamerlane portraits from life survive, but written accounts agree that he was lean, muscular, and broad shouldered, with a large head and deep-set, penetrating eyes.

imperial line of Genghis, and he never called himself khan.

As soon as he became master of Transoxiana, Tamerlane ordered the execution of the puppet khan Kabul-Shah. Although this hapless holy man had been installed as khan by both Tamerlane and Husayn, he had supported Husayn against Tamerlane, effectively signing his own death warrant. Still, Tamerlane knew he needed a member of the royal family as khan for the sake of appearances, so he tactfully found another descendant of Genghis to accept the title.

Tamerlane seized the treasures Husayn had collected over the years and distributed them among his generals and amirs. After making his own choices from his predecessor's harem, he handed out the rest of the women to his men. Making it clear whose family ruled, he then had Husayn's two young sons executed; their bodies were burned and their ashes scattered in the wind.

With Samarkand secure as the center of his kingdom, Tamerlane now set out to conquer the surrounding territories. His immediate aims were to obtain booty and to prevent any rival kingdoms from threatening his own. His great ambition was to reestablish the vast, fragmented empire of Genghis Khan and, like that great Mongol conqueror, to rule the East.

To the northwest was Khwarizm, the kingdom once ruled by Genghis Khan's grandson Batu. To the east was Mogulistan, the land of the Jats. Mogulistan, the country of Genghis's son Chagatai, had originally included Transoxiana. Its inhabitants, the *Moguls*, were nomads who rode free through the entire land. The Moguls, who considered themselves lords of the old empire, despised the settled people around them. The word *mogul* has come down to our time with the meaning of "powerful or influential person."

Tamerlane considered both Khwarizm and Mogulistan threats to his borders. Both were rich, tempting lands. He eyed them hungrily, and for two decades he devoted much of his energy to making war with them.

A 13th-century Persian carving shows a camel-mounted warrior riding into the desert with a woman captive. Regarded as property to be bought, sold, traded, or stolen, the women of Tamerlane's world had almost no voice in their own destinies.

First he attacked Mogulistan. This land had been ruled by Tughlugh-Timur and, after his death, by his son Ilyas-Khoja. Ilyas, who with his army of Jats had been driven from the walls of Samarkand in 1365, had been assassinated soon afterward. In 1370 Tamerlane began a series of expeditions against Ilyas's successor, Kamar-ad-Din. The first attack put the new khan to flight and supplied the invading forces with rich plunder.

Tamerlane's next major thrust against Mogulistan came in 1375. In this campaign Tamerlane's son Jahangir scattered Kamar-ad-Din's forces and pursued the khan deep into the mountains. The khan escaped, but Tamerlane captured his daughter, whom he added to his harem. Tamerlane would continue to wage intermittent warfare against Kamar-ad-Din until 1390, when the Jat leader, once again put to flight, finally vanished for good.

In between his attacks on Mogulistan, Tamerlane turned his attention to neighboring Khwarizm. In 1372 he sent an ambassador to the kingdom's ruler, known as the *sufi*, demanding Khwarizm's southern provinces. Predictably, the sufi refused; equally predictably, Tamerlane mobilized his army and attacked. The fighting was heavy, but the Tartar army at last conquered the important city of Kat, slaughtering its male citizens and carrying off its women and children as slaves.

Apparently ready to concede defeat, the sufi, Yusuf, offered his niece, the celebrated beauty Khan-Zada, as a bride for Tamerlane's son Jahangir. Tamerlane accepted this peace overture and took his army back to his own capital, Samarkand. The sufi, however, regretted his move. Refusing to send Khan-Zada to Samarkand as he had promised, he reoccupied Kat and attacked Tamerlane's border settlements.

Tamerlane was always ready to fight if he was defied, and he never really trusted any victory he had not won by force of arms. He mobilized his troops at once and marched toward Khwarizm. This time Yusuf saw the light. He sent Khan-Zada to Jahangir in a dazzling caravan loaded with jewels and gold, priceless carpets and tapestries.

Despite his capture by the Persians, a Tartar warrior retains his proud, self-confident expression. Almost always successful in battle, the soldiers of the Mongol armies were famed for their ferocity and courage.

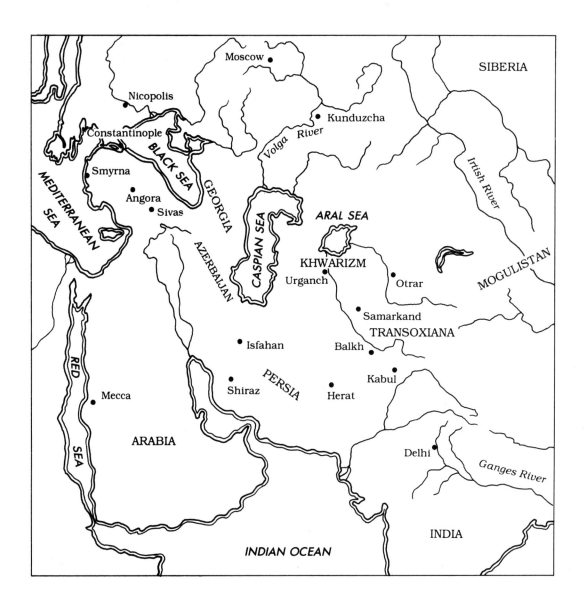

The map shows cities and regions including Moscow, Nicopolis, Constantinople, Smyrna, Angora, Sivas, Mecca, Shiraz, Isfahan, Urganch, Samarkand, Balkh, Herat, Kabul, Delhi, and the seas and rivers: MEDITERRANEAN SEA, BLACK SEA, CASPIAN SEA, ARAL SEA, RED SEA, INDIAN OCEAN, Volga River, Irtish River, Ganges River, and regions SIBERIA, GEORGIA, AZERBAIJAN, KHWARIZM, TRANSOXIANA, MOGULISTAN, PERSIA, ARABIA, INDIA. Kunduzcha and Otrar are also marked.

Tamerlane hoped to reestablish and enlarge the Mongol empire created by Genghis Khan. Although he was never to conquer China, Tamerlane's armies swept across Asia from Mongolia to the Mediterranean Sea, and from Moscow to Delhi.

The princess, a descendant of Genghis Khan, was married to Jahangir in an elaborate ceremony in 1373. The following year the 38-year-old Tamerlane became a grandfather for the first time when Jahangir and Khan-Zada had a son, Muhammad-Sultan. Jahangir had always been his father's favorite, and his son would prove to be equally close to Tamerlane, who eventually made Muhammad-Sultan his heir.

Tamerlane's delight in his son's marriage was not to last. When the Tartar chief departed for a campaign in Mogulistan in 1375, Jahangir was ill and remained in Samarkand. When Tamerlane returned, the city was in deep grief. Jahangir, 20 years old, was dead. Tough and battle hardened though he was, Tamerlane was devastated by the loss of his firstborn son. For months, he wore only the traditional mourning colors of blue and black, covered his head with dust, and beat his breast in sorrow.

Affairs of state, however, had to proceed. According to custom, the young widow Khan-Zada was given in marriage to Tamerlane's third son, Miran-Shah. Tamerlane's grief was lightened by the birth of a second grandson, Pir-Muhammad, born to another wife of Jahangir a month after the young man's death.

Khwarizm, which had remained quiet for some time after the marriage of its princess to Tamerlane's son, once again rose in revolt in 1379. The Tartar army again marched to the north, this time laying siege to its capital, the city of Urganch.

Yusuf, the sufi, knew his defending army could not resist Tamerlane's desert warriors for long. In desperation, he challenged Tamerlane to personal combat, winner take all. The lame Tartar accepted the challenge gladly, over the protests of his generals, and rode out onto the field with his shield and scimitar ready for the fight.

It was the right decision. Yusuf never appeared, and Tamerlane, with a rare loud laugh, called his men to attack the city. According to one chronicler, the sufi was so terrified that he became sick and died almost at once. The city submitted without further struggle, and Khwarizm duly became a province of Transoxiana.

With relentless regularity, Tamerlane went from battle to battle, ceaselessly widening his dominion in all directions. His pattern of conquest was always the same. He would begin by demanding submission of the local lord or king. Those who refused, or later rebelled, were mercilessly crushed by an army that daily grew larger and more efficient.

> *Tamerlane was unlettered but not ignorant. His physical vigor was matched by his mental vitality. He delighted in the company of scholars, and with them mastered many subjects.*
> —HILDA HOOKHAM
> British historian

Their armor glinting in the sun, Persian cavalrymen throw their weight against Tamerlane's onrushing warriors. The Persians were valiant soldiers, but they were outridden and outnumbered by the mighty Mongol horde from Samarkand.

A page from a 13th-century Koran exhibits the elaborate decorative style of the period. The Koran — the holy book of Islam—contains the basis of Muslim religion and law.

Tamerlane's soldiers came from every kingdom he subdued. In addition to the many tribes of Tartars — Barlas and Jats and Jalairs and a hundred others — there were Turks and Persians, Arabs and Afghans, fighting side by side, all obedient to their lord. Together they dominated and controlled the wild plains of central Asia.

Modern eyes tend to see Tamerlane's troops as a wild-eyed mob, more a gang of marauders than a disciplined army. In fact, his army was organized with as much control and order as any modern military force. Like the legions of Genghis Khan almost 200 years before them, Tamerlane's men were divided into ranks of cavalry and infantry, with a specialized corps of engineers for sieges. And, like the great khan's army, they were trained and drilled to act together with such unity that they were virtually invincible.

But there were differences in the strategy of the two conquerors, differences that reflected the changed conditions and terrain of their wars. Genghis's armies had always depended on the inspired horsemanship of the Mongols, using the cavalry to crush their enemy in the first attack. Tamerlane's greatest innovation was a reversal of the old Mongol's tactic, using the infantry to take

Persian craftsmen were celebrated for their elaborately decorated iron stirrups and other harness equipment. The products of Persia's artisans, which also included armor, enamelwork, and richly patterned carpets, were in demand throughout Asia in Tamerlane's time.

The wealth of Persia, which included such gorgeously decorated buildings as this mosque in the city of Isfahan, presented an irresistible temptation to Tamerlane. He set out to conquer and loot the ancient kingdom in 1380.

the first shock and holding the more maneuverable cavalry for the point in the battle when the enemy was in disorder.

Tamerlane was a diplomat as well as a warrior. When he defeated the chieftain of a territory, he often reinstated him as its vassal governor. When local lords were killed or refused to cooperate, the conquered territories were put under the command of Tamerlane's sons or trusted officers. Each area he subdued served as a further protection from attack. All through the 1370s he extended his rule and reinforced his control.

As masterful as he was on the battlefield, Tamerlane never attempted to establish a central government or a uniform code of law, as Genghis Khan had. And he never won, or tried to win, the love or loyalty of his defeated enemies. Conquered tribes rebelled as soon as Tamerlane's men rode on, and he had to return again and again to subdue them.

Gradually, however, the indomitable power of Tamerlane's armies began to discourage the quarrelsome and independent tribes of central Asia, and the loosely organized kingdoms of Khwarizm and Mogulistan — covering land that now represents parts of China, the Soviet Union, and Afghanistan — came to accept the supremacy of the lame Tartar from Transoxiana. It took nine expeditions, four to Khwarizm and five to Mogulistan, to subdue these kingdoms completely, but by the end of the decade, in 1380, Tamerlane sat securely on his throne.

In his 44 years, Tamerlane had risen to great heights, but it is only from this point in his life that historians measure his career as a world figure. "His reign . . . only really begins," according to the *Encyclopedia of Islam*, "with the conquest of Mogulistan and Khwarizm."

When Tamerlane was crowned in 1370, he proclaimed himself the successor of Genghis's son Chagatai. In the decade that followed, he made good that boast, reassembling Chagatai's kingdom piece by piece and bringing it all under his command. He was now indeed the great lord of all central Asia. But he was still not satisfied.

In 1380 he turned his eyes southward, looking

toward the rich kingdom of Persia. Although it had never been a part of Genghis's empire, Persia had been conquered a century earlier by Genghis's grandson. Tamerlane's decision to conquer it was a fateful one, both for himself and for Asia. Some historians consider it the greatest mistake of his life. It was certainly the turning point.

In his *A Study of History*, British scholar Arnold Toynbee argued that Tamerlane's Persian adventures "broke the back of his own Transoxiana by squandering on aimless expeditions . . . the slender reserves of Transoxianian strength . . . [Tamerlane] devoted almost the whole of the last 24 years of his life to a series of barren and destructive campaigns."

Not all historians agree with Toynbee's negative view of Tamerlane's career. Many believe that 1380 was the start of the most glorious period of his life. It was in this year that he ceased to see himself merely as the great lord of Transoxiana and began to take the world view that was to make him a historical figure comparable to Alexander the Great, Julius Caesar, and Genghis Khan.

Alexander the Great rides into battle against the Persian army. Tamerlane's path of conquest followed much the same route as that traveled by the mighty Greek leader 17 centuries earlier.

65

4

Conqueror

During the decade Tamerlane spent establishing his power in Transoxiana and conquering the kingdoms around it, he made few mistakes, either on the battlefield or in his court. He did, however, make one serious error of judgment that would cost him dearly in the years to follow. It occurred in 1376, when he was asked for help by a prince of the imperial family of Genghis Khan.

When Genghis died in 1227, his empire was divided into two main sections. The largest was known as the Golden Horde, the other as the White Horde. By the last third of the 14th century, the once powerful and unified Golden Horde, now ruled by an amir named Mamai, had been severely weakened by civil and foreign war. The White Horde had meanwhile been growing stronger; its khan, Urus, was eager to increase his power and to take control of the Golden Horde.

Tamerlane, whose own lands bordered those of the White Horde, had no intention of permitting Urus to become so strong. Furthermore, he hoped to conquer the Golden Horde himself at some time in the future. By 1376 he was considering the best

> *As there is only one god in heaven, so should there be only one monarch on earth.*
> —TAMERLANE

Like many world leaders of whom no authentic portrait exists, Tamerlane has been portrayed through the centuries as many different men, each reflecting the artist's own time and place. The unknown European illustrator who created this likeness saw the Mongol warrior as a knight in the Western romantic tradition.

Almost a quarter of a million Russian infantrymen like this one died during Toktamish's victorious 1382 campaign against the Christian princes of Russia. Leading the united forces of the Golden and White Hordes, Toktamish burned every building in his path, giving special attention to Christian churches.

way to put a stop to the ambitious khan's plans. At this point one of Urus's royal kinsmen, a prince named Toktamish, appeared at Tamerlane's court. Toktamish's father had been killed while trying to seize power from Urus, and Toktamish now sought Tamerlane's aid in securing the throne for himself.

Tamerlane took him in, delighted to have a noble of the line of Genghis Khan in his debt. He had known that eventually he would have to meet Urus in battle; here was a chance to let a prince of the royal house do it for him. Toktamish swore loyalty to Tamerlane, who heaped honor upon his guest, providing him with tents and camels, slaves and soldiers, weapons and horses.

Thus equipped, Toktamish took to the field against Urus. He led several attacks on the khan's forces, each of them ending in defeat, although one of Urus's sons was killed during a battle with Toktamish's forces. After each unsuccessful attempt, Tamerlane gave his new ally fresh horses, more soldiers, and increased encouragement.

Understandably worried about Toktamish's alliance with his powerful neighbor, Urus sent envoys to Tamerlane with a message: "Toktamish killed my son and has taken refuge in your territory. Give up to me my enemy. If not, prepare for battle!" For Tamerlane, the excuse to measure swords against Urus, especially with a royal prince at his side to give his cause legitimacy, was welcome. He replied that he was ready.

In late 1376 Tamerlane, Toktamish at his side, led his army against Urus. This time the forces of the White Horde met a resounding defeat. The warfare was stalled by an unusually severe winter that virtually paralyzed both sides, but in the spring Tamerlane equipped Toktamish to resume the assault. Urus had died during the winter, but his armies, led by his sons, once again vanquished Toktamish. Finally, still aided by Tamerlane, Toktamish achieved victory. He installed himself as khan of the White Horde in 1378.

If Tamerlane had expected gratitude or loyalty from Toktamish, he must have been bitterly disappointed by the next series of events. Instead of joining Tamerlane in his efforts to conquer the Golden Horde, Toktamish set out to master it himself. He picked the right time to do it. Mamai, the khan of the Golden Horde, had just suffered a stunning defeat at the hands of his former vassals in what is now western Russia. Toktamish and the White Horde attacked Mamai's weakened forces and, in 1380, overwhelmed them.

Toktamish was now khan of the united White and Golden Hordes. He established a capital on the Volga River and called on the Russian princes to pay tribute and recognize his sovereignty. When they refused, he mobilized his now huge armies and mounted an attack. Exhausted by their long and bloody war with Mamai, the Russians were no match for this new wave of Mongols, and Toktamish's advance was almost unimpeded. "Columns of smoke and fire from the flaming crops and villages heralded by day and night the approach of the Mongolian army," wrote an observer.

Toktamish marched on to Moscow, which he burned to the ground in 1382. After the royal family of Russia submitted, Toktamish held their dead for ransom. He demanded payment of one ruble (a silver coin) for every 80 fallen soldiers the Russians wished to bury. He was said to have collected 3,000 rubles from the survivors of the battle of Moscow in return for their 240,000 dead.

The Russian princes agreed to pay annual tribute to Toktamish. As a descendant of the mighty Genghis and thus a legitimate heir to the throne of the Golden Horde, he had coins struck in his name as ruler of the region. Certainly, he must have reasoned, he owed nothing to an upstart like Tamerlane, who had no royal blood. Tamerlane's title was still only great lord of Transoxiana, and even that honor had been appropriated from Genghis's legitimate heirs.

Toktamish had probably never intended to honor his promise of allegiance to his benefactor; now, as the ruler of Russian princes and lord of the great Golden Horde, he had no intention of permitting Tamerlane to rule kingdoms that by rights belonged to the line of Genghis. His path was certain: he

The just Khan, the Helper of Religion and of the World.
—inscription on coins minted by Toktamish

The Masjid-Jami mosque in Herat, Afghanistan, was built by Tamerlane's son Shah-Rukh. Herat, an important commercial hub for centuries, was ravaged by Genghis Khan in 1222 and again by Tamerlane in 1380; under the Mongol chief's successors, however, the city became a brilliant center of Islamic culture.

Now acclaimed as a masterpiece, this delicate painting from Herat, showing a man holding a spray of flowers, survived Tamerlane's assault. Herat, a major city in modern Afghanistan, is celebrated for its fine carpets.

would reconquer Transoxiana and Persia.

Tamerlane's first major expedition into Persia, in 1380, had been against Herat, a rich city in what is now Afghanistan. His men had looted Herat of its gold and jewels, and they wrested the giant bronze doors of the city from their hinges and sent them to Transoxiana. When Herat rebelled after its surrender, Tamerlane returned, suppressed the revolt, and had towers built of the skulls of its slaughtered inhabitants.

The history of the next few years reveals an uninterrupted series of the atrocities with which Tamerlane sought to terrorize the people of Persia into submission. In 1387, for example, he conquered the beautiful and wealthy city of Isfahan and demanded a gigantic payment to leave it in peace. Rioting in protest, the city's people killed 3,000 of Tamerlane's troops. Tamerlane reacted with the calm of a businessman, ordering his men to collect 70,000 heads as a reprisal.

Historian Michael Prawdin describes the scene in *The Mongol Empire*: "Even in Tamerlane's army there were soldiers whose gorge rose at the thought of decapitating unresisting persons, and many preferred to buy a head from some less scrupulous comrade. In this army, overladen with spoils, money was cheap, so the price was fixed at one gold piece per head. But the supply so greatly exceeded the demand that the price of a head fell to half a gold piece, and soon no one would buy any more human heads. Tamerlane was supplied with the 70,000 he demanded, and they were piled in pyramids along the top of the wall."

The conqueror swept from city to city, seizing what he wanted and installing his officers as governors to collect tribute. His reputation preceded him, and he encountered little resistance. When he did meet opposition, however, he was merciless.

In the rebellious city of Sabzawar, in present-day Afghanistan, he had a tower built out of 2,000 live prisoners, stacked on top of each other and cemented together with bricks and mortar. His own court historian reported proudly that in Sivas, in what is now Turkey, he promised the populace that if they surrendered peacefully, not one drop of their blood would be shed. When the defenders of the city opened the gates, he had 4,000 of them buried alive. Tamerlane kept his promises.

Not every report of Tamerlane's conquests includes such appalling violence. When, for example, he had conquered Shirvan, in what is now the southern Soviet Union, the city's king brought him an array of magnificent gifts in tribute — jewels, robes, golden ornaments, and slaves. The collection included nine (a sacred number) of each item but

> *My valiant soldiers have no other duty than the trade of war. They are lions, who, instead of living in forests, have their residence in camps and armies.*
> —TAMERLANE

one; there were only eight slaves. When Tamerlane demanded an explanation of this insult, the king knelt at the conqueror's feet; he himself, he said, was the ninth slave. Delighted by the gesture, Tamerlane showered the vanquished king with gifts and restored him to his throne.

By 1386 Tamerlane held most of the area now comprising Iran, Afghanistan, and Turkey, as well as much of Russia. Still, there was no escaping the confrontation that was coming with his rival in the north. Just as he had not been able to ascend the throne of Transoxiana without dealing with Husayn, he could not extend his territory in central and northern Asia without resolving the issue with Toktamish.

In early 1387 Tamerlane and his army were still in their winter quarters in Azerbaijan (now in the southern Soviet Union) when Toktamish sent his army across the mountains to attack them. The first skirmish went to Tamerlane, whose son Miran-Shah turned the tide of battle and took some of Toktamish's highest-ranking officers prisoner.

Still the diplomat — or perhaps simply unwilling to believe that a man he had befriended could turn on him so coldly — Tamerlane freed the prisoners and sent them back to the khan with a message: "Why is it that you, a prince whom I look upon as my son, should without cause overrun this land and try to bring thousands of fellow Muslims to destruction? You should henceforward avoid such unseemly behavior."

The letter, which made it clear that Tamerlane still considered the mighty khan his vassal, must have infuriated Toktamish. In any case, its fatherly tone left him unmoved; he continued with his plans to seize Tamerlane's domains and to rid the East of this man he considered a presumptuous thief of Genghis's legacy.

Determined to strike at the heart of his rival, Toktamish soon marched into Transoxiana, where he laid waste the countryside. By now — in late 1387 — he had the support of many of Tamerlane's old enemies; the sufis of Khwarizm and the Jat nobles of Mogulistan were delighted to join anyone who threatened their conqueror. The Lord of the Fortunate Conjunction was beset from all sides. His power, his conquests, his very existence, were now threatened with obliteration by one of the few people to whom he had shown kindness.

Tamerlane was still in Persia when word of Toktamish's devastating raids on Transoxiana reached him in February 1388. He began the long march home, but by the time he reached Samarkand, Toktamish had withdrawn his forces. The Golden Horde attacked Transoxiana again in late 1388; Tamerlane repelled the invasion, but the winter's bitter cold and blinding snowstorms kept him from pursuing his enemy beyond the country's borders.

Rather than remain in a defensive position at home, Tamerlane resolved to pursue Toktamish into his own territory. Before setting out, he sent troops to various parts of his realm to punish those who had joined forces with the Golden Horde. He attacked the Jats, burning and looting their territory to prevent another uprising. Then he headed back to Samarkand to prepare for the epic battle with Toktamish.

Finally, in January 1391, Tamerlane led his army, said to number 200,000 men, north toward the icy plains of Siberia. Freezing and hungry, they had marched more than 1,000 miles by the time they caught up with the fleeing Golden Horde southeast

A pair of carved dragon heads face each other across the top of a jade sword handle from Persia. Tamerlane's men carried tons of Persian loot home to Transoxiana.

The Persian city of Isfahan saw a brisk trade in human heads after Tamerlane demanded 70,000 such trophies. A handful of residents managed to hide on the day of the slaughter. They tried to escape that night, but it had begun to snow; following their tracks, Tamerlane's men caught and killed them.

of Moscow. The two titanic armies came face-to-face at last at Kunduzcha, near the Volga River.

The advantage seemed to be with the Golden Horde: they were northerners, accustomed to cold weather and to winter fighting; they were in their own territory; their horses, bred in the north, knew how to find food beneath the snow. Above all, Toktamish's forces, which far outnumbered Tamerlane's, were well fed and well rested. Tamerlane was counting on the fact that Toktamish would not expect a winter attack from him; he had tracked him into his own country precisely to surprise him there.

Tamerlane's army was a mercenary force that depended on loot and the rewards of valor. A regular soldier received the value of a horse if he survived, twice that if he showed bravery; an officer who led 10 men was awarded 10 times as much, and so on. A brave or skillful soldier could make himself rich. This was the motive for Tamerlane's hard-pressed forces that winter; the plunder of the Golden Horde would support a good soldier for life—if he lived.

Before leading his men into battle, Tamerlane, as was his custom, stretched himself full-length on the ground, praying for victory. As he rose, the Muslim battle cry, *Allah Akbar!* ("God is great!") roared from 200,000 throats. Sparks seemed to fly as the sun struck thousands of glittering swords, shields, coats of armor, and highly polished, plume-crested helmets. War trumpets blasted, drums thundered, and the army moved forward.

"Then," reported a witness, "the wolves of war set their teeth. . . . Leaders and common soldiers alike plunged into seas of blood and arrows." The two armies fought for three days. It was a confrontation unparalleled in the history of the East. Time after time, Tamerlane's military standard — a lance topped with a horsetail — sank and seemed ready to fall; time after time it rose again as the tireless warrior rallied his troops.

On the third day of the battle, Toktamish's men had worked themselves into a position behind Tamerlane's; from here they mounted a fierce attack. The Tartar chief, who had been in pursuit of the Golden Horde's main force, reined up and led his

The earth became a cloud of dust, and was transformed into a raging sea whose threatening waves washed hither and thither. The sun, the source of light, was darkened by the dust thrown up by the furious riders, and the countenance of the moon was soiled by the dust. The heavenly sphere emitted a long-drawn groan, and the world plaintively petitioned for grace.
—contemporary chronicle of the Battle of Kunduzcha

cavalry to the rear, dispersing the attackers.

Then, as the soldiers of the Golden Horde watched in horror, their own horned standard sank to the earth, the traditional sign of the death of the king. Believing Toktamish dead, they panicked and took to the woods. Toktamish was very much alive. Furious but helpless, he could do nothing but flee with his troops.

Tamerlane must have smiled to see the success of the most desperate ruse of his career: during a heavy rainstorm before the battle, he had bribed the standard-bearer of the Golden Horde, paying him richly to lower the khan's standard at Tamerlane's signal. As he had known they would, Toktamish's men, with no time to think, had simply bolted.

Like Napoleon and Hitler after him, Tamerlane paid dearly for his invasion of Russia; more than 100,000 of his men lay dead on the blood-soaked field of battle. But unlike the later invaders, Tamerlane won. When Toktamish's proud standard fell, trick though it was, it fell for good. The khan escaped with his life, but he was never able to raise a great army again.

Toktamish resurfaces in history four years later, when he rallied enough men to try another attack on Tamerlane, but that confrontation — the Battle of Terek in 1395 — was his last. Tamerlane so shattered the Golden Horde in this battle that it ceased to be a serious threat. One observer who knew Tamerlane well said that of all the Tartar chief's triumphs, his victory over Toktamish was the one he most prized.

In January 1405 Tamerlane received envoys from Toktamish, now powerless and repentant. His message to Tamerlane said, "I have suffered the punishment I deserve for my ingratitude. . . . If I am forgiven, then my head will never move from the yoke of submission, nor my foot from the path of obedience."

In spite of the fierce and protracted warfare between the two, Tamerlane had never wholly lost his affection for his onetime protégé. He promised to help him, but time had run out. Some historians believe that the following year Toktamish was murdered by his own brother, who had succeeded him on the shaky throne of the Golden Horde.

The Battle of Kunduzcha provided Tamerlane's men with enough plunder to make up for all the pain and danger they had suffered; every survivor of the struggle was rich. For nearly a month they feasted, drank wine from golden cups, and listened to ballads of victory, celebrating in Russia's desolate wastelands.

A minaret soars into the sky above Isfahan. Part of a mosque, a minaret is a tower from which the Muslim *muezzin*, or crier, calls the faithful to prayer many times a day. When Tamerlane left Isfahan, the city had several new minarets — made from human skulls.

5

Earthshaker

Tamerlane returned to his capital, Samarkand, in late 1392. It was almost two years since he had left to fight Toktamish, and his people greeted him with wild excitement. After a round of riotous celebratory feasts, Tamerlane moved his court to the meadowlands north of the city. Joined there by his army's heavily laden baggage trains, he distributed loot and slaves he had captured from Toktamish among his wives, other family members, and courtiers.

Tamerlane never really had a permanent home. It was truly said of him that he "lived in the saddle." He had made Samarkand the most splendid city in Asia with the plunder of a hundred campaigns, but he rarely spent more than a few days in the city, much preferring his camp outside its walls.

For the next five years, Tamerlane and his men rode from city to city across his wide dominions, fighting for more land and more loot, fighting to restore order, and fighting to punish those who defied Tartar rule. Although the sword was seldom out of Tamerlane's hand, he thought of himself as a man of peace and always insisted that those who fell before his invincible armies had brought their destruction on themselves.

If I were alive today, mankind would tremble!
—inscription on Tamerlane's tomb

Tamerlane returns to Samarkand after his 1391 victory over Toktamish. Every man in the Mongol leader's army came home rich; many, in fact, had collected so much treasure from Toktamish's immense entourage that they had to abandon some of it on Russia's windy steppes.

When he attacked a city, it was his custom to raise a white flag on the first day of the siege; this indicated that if the city surrendered at once, its residents would be spared. On the second day, the white flag was replaced by a red one, which meant that the city's ruler and its leading citizens would be executed. If the city held out for a third day, a black flag flew over Tamerlane's tent. This meant that everyone in the city—soldier and civilian, young and old, man and woman — would be killed without appeal.

He was seldom opposed, so fearsome had his name become, but when an army was rash enough to offer him combat, the results were always dreadful. In 1393 he attacked Shiraz, a Persian city he had conquered several years earlier. In his absence a Persian prince, Shah-Mansur, had seized power; now Tamerlane's object was the capture and punishment of the usurper.

When Tamerlane approached Shiraz with 30,000 men, Shah-Mansur met him outside the city with a force numbering fewer than 4,000. Tamerlane, unworried by Mansur's impending attack, had made no defensive plans, and the small Persian force galloped straight into the center of the Tartar encampment. "Shah-Mansur advanced at their head," wrote a witness, "like a furious lion."

The astonished Tamerlane suddenly found himself face-to-face with Mansur, who raised his sword and struck the Tartar chief on the head. Tamerlane was protected from injury by his heavy helmet, but Mansur was wounded by the Tartar guards. The Persian prince fled with his surviving troops, Tamerlane's youngest son, Shah-Rukh, in hot pursuit. The 16-year-old Shah-Rukh, according to a contemporary chronicler, returned with Mansur's head, which he placed at his father's feet. "May the heads of all your enemies," said the boy, "be laid at your feet like the head of the proud Mansur."

The remainder of Mansur's soldiers were quickly slaughtered, and Tamerlane reentered Shiraz in triumph. Mansur became a legendary hero; the saga of his reckless courage is still told in story and song in the Mideast.

Tamerlane's military success depended most heavily on his army's superb mounted archers. A man entering the Mongol leader's cavalry was required to bring with him a horse, a bow, 30 arrows, an ax, and a cooking pot. The richer enlistees wore armor, but common soldiers dressed in leather.

83

Magnificent examples of Tamerlane's buildings, like this many-chambered palace, still stand in Samarkand. The city's major structures were built of baked bricks, covered on the outside with brilliantly colored tile mosaics. The interior walls — almost none of which survive — were elaborately painted with dragons, birds, and battle scenes.

A wall plaque from Delhi. Elephants were popular subjects with India's artists and craftsmen — and with India's Mongol conquerors. Tamerlane was especially proud of the war elephants he took from India; the great beasts played a starring role in the parades he held to celebrate his return to Samarkand.

Tamerlane's next prey was Iraq, a small, ancient kingdom that fell easily in 1393. The Tartar troops, according to a contemporary writer, "hurled themselves upon Iraq like armies of ants and grasshoppers; they overran the countryside and sped in all directions, plundering and ravaging."

Pushing north, Tamerlane attacked the province of Kurdistan. Here he lost his second son, Omar-Sheik, who fell to one of the defenders' arrows. For all his displays of cruelty and lack of regard for human life, Tamerlane, like most men, loved his children dearly. He was crushed by Omar-Sheik's death. Witnesses reported, however, that he received the news without even changing his expression. Omar-Sheik's body was carried back to Transoxiana, there to be interred with his brother Jahangir.

Georgia, an independent kingdom in what is now the Soviet Union, succumbed after Tamerlane destroyed 700 of its villages and all of its Christian churches and ruined most of its cultivated land. Following his 1395 encounter with Toktamish, Tamerlane returned to Samarkand.

Now almost 60 years old, he took the longest break between campaigns he had ever allowed himself. For two years he stayed home, directing the construction of vast and imposing buildings to beautify Samarkand. He had picked this city to represent his empire, and he intended to make it the finest capital in the world.

Samarkand was a large, sophisticated city. It was, even by the standards of our own century, a comfortable and elegant place to live. Within its walls were 150,000 people; probably twice that number lived in its surrounding suburbs. A visitor might first notice the city's innumerable mosques, its gorgeously decorated palaces, its religious shrines adorned with mosaics and crowned with glittering blue domes. Perhaps more impressive still, however, was Samarkand's lush greenery.

Nourished by piped-in water, trees grew everywhere, shading the streets and houses of this desert city. More than a dozen gigantic, elaborately designed gardens adorned Samarkand. Tamerlane's

When God wills something He furnishes the causes by which it may be brought about according to His providence. To Tamerlane and his posterity, He had destined the empire of Asia, foreseeing the mildness of his rule, which would bring happiness to his subjects.
—NIZAM AL-DIN SHAMI
14th-century historian

History repeated itself in 1526, when the war elephants of Delhi's defending army were vanquished by a Mongol invasion force. This time the attackers were led by the Mongol conqueror Babur, Tamerlane's great-great-great-grandson. Babur went on to found a dynasty of Muslim emperors who ruled India until 1857.

gardens — one of which was said to be 100 miles long — were filled with flowers, fruit trees, fish ponds, marble pavilions, and great sweeps of emerald lawns. When he was away from the city — as he usually was — he allowed its residents to use his gardens as public parks.

The city was copiously supplied with water, which was delivered by canals and a complex network of pipes. Each house had its own water supply, and the city was dotted with pools and reservoirs. Rich citizens offered public ice-water fountains, of which there were said to be more than 2,000.

Whenever Tamerlane conquered a city, he took away its artists, builders, and craftsmen. Samarkand was home to thousands of these displaced creators, whose arts were applied to increase the city's magnificence. One of Samarkand's most impressive features was its marketplace — a broad highway through the middle of the city, its sides lined with shops — which Tamerlane completed in 1404. The entire bazaar was covered by a vaulted, glass-windowed roof.

Samarkand's citizens ate well. "Bread is everywhere," reported one visitor, "and rice can be had cheap in any quantity." The city's bakeries and restaurants were celebrated. Stalls all over the city sold roasted meat, and vegetables and fruit were plentiful. In Samarkand, noted an admiring Chinese traveler, the watermelons were often "as large as a horse's head."

During the two years—1396–98—that Tamerlane spent in Samarkand, he was working on more than civic improvement; he was also planning his biggest expedition to date: the conquest of India. The 1398 invasion of this fabled land was the shortest and bloodiest campaign of Tamerlane's career. It was also one of the most profitable. Six months after he had left for Delhi, Tamerlane returned to Samarkand with his immense cargo of gold, slaves, and elephants.

While he was in India, Tamerlane had received a disturbing letter from his oldest surviving son, Miran-Shah, whom he had installed as governor of northern Persia. Inexplicably ignoring the Muslim

tradition of deep respect for one's father, Miran-Shah had called Tamerlane too old to rule and had bitterly criticized his behavior. "You go forward," said Miran-Shah, "but on a crooked road." This was bad enough, but when the aging conqueror returned to Samarkand, he heard rumors about Miran-Shah that distressed him even more.

The young man was said to be behaving in a most unroyal way. He had retreated in battle, destroyed

A 14th-century manuscript depicts Islam's founder, the prophet Muhammad (tall figure in white), with his family. The Muslim faith emphasizes respect for one's father; the devout Tamerlane was thus particularly offended when his son Miran-Shah criticized him.

The ruins of an imposing mosque in Turkey give silent testimony to the strength of that nation's Muslim faith. Tamerlane had always said he went to war to destroy "infidels" (non-Muslims). When it seemed necessary to attack the Muslim Ottoman Turks, however, he managed to forget his religious objectives.

tombs, wasted the imperial treasury, and even ordered the execution of a Muslim holy man, an act the devout Tamerlane would have found unthinkable. Furthermore, Miran-Shah was reportedly drinking heavily and spending his days gambling with unsavory companions.

Tamerlane soon received an urgent visit from Khan-Zada, the princess who had married Miran-Shah at the death of her first husband, Tamerlane's son Jahangir. Khan-Zada confirmed the rumors, adding that her husband was badly mistreating her. Furious, Tamerlane set out for Sultaniya, Miran-Shah's capital, in 1399.

There the charges against Miran-Shah were investigated; the outcome was the execution of those men held to have "corrupted" the son of the Tartar chief. Miran-Shah and his father had a long meeting; what was said, reported one observer, "none but Allah can unfold." In any case, Tamerlane evidently forgave his erring son, whose brain, some said, had been injured when he fell from a horse. Miran-Shah remained at his father's side for the rest of the conqueror's life.

Soon after he had set matters straight with Miran-Shah, Tamerlane set out on what was probably his greatest campaign, one that made his expeditions to Persia, Russia, and even India seem like minor confrontations. It was this campaign that, even more than his defeat of Toktamish, earned him the name "Earthshaker." Tamerlane's 1402 march against the Ottoman Turks was to change the history of Europe no less than that of Asia. It spread the dread name of the lame Mongol chieftain around the world.

Until now Tamerlane's conquests had, for the most part, been easy ones. "In Central Asia, in Persia, and in India," observes British historian P. C. Sykes, Tamerlane "had encountered no formidable state ruled by a warlike monarch, and with his large numbers, perfect discipline, and vast experience, victory must have become a matter of course." The empire of the Ottoman Turks was to be quite another story.

> Notwithstanding the Smyrna massacre, Tamerlane's triumph over Bayazid saved Christendom.
> —RENÉ GROUSSET
> French historian

The Ottoman Turks were descended from a Turkish tribe that had escaped from Genghis Khan and created a powerful kingdom in Anatolia (an area that included present-day Turkey). They were, like Tamerlane and his army, Muslims. Led by their mighty sultan, Bayazid — known as *Yilderim*, or "the Thunderbolt," because of the speed and brilliance of his military maneuvers — they had repeatedly faced and defeated the Christians of Europe, seizing province after province. Under Bayazid's leadership, the Ottoman Turks had also vastly increased their holdings around Asia Minor (present-day Turkey).

In 1396 Bayazid had wiped out a 100,000-man army composed of French, English, Flemish, and German nobles. This huge force had attempted to put a stop to his advances into Christian Europe. By 1400 his empire stretched into Europe as far north as Hungary and across Asia Minor to the boundaries of Tamerlane's own provinces in Armenia. Bayazid was now preparing to seize Constantinople (now Istanbul, in Turkey), the center of eastern Christianity. If any leader rivaled Tamerlane the Earthshaker, it was undoubtedly Bayazid the Thunderbolt.

In Tamerlane's eyes, there could be only one world conqueror. When Bayazid demanded tribute from a prince who was under Tamerlane's protection, the Tartar sent the Turk a letter full of lush Oriental insults and rich rhetorical threats. Since Tamerlane never learned to read or write, one of his court scribes must have written the letter for him, but its ripe contempt and bravado obviously reflected the Earthshaker's feelings.

Tamerlane told Bayazid that he had only tolerated him until then because they were fellow Muslims; the "Turcoman" had better not forget that he was only an ant, whereas he, Tamerlane, was an elephant. No one, said the Tartar, had ever challenged his armies and survived. "Fate," he assured Bayazid, "protects our empire."

The Turkish sultan replied in kind: his letter began, "O ravening dog named Tamerlane." He went on to say, "It is long since we have desired to make

war upon you. Thanks be to God and the Prophet our desire is about to be fulfilled, for we have resolved to march against you. . . . If you refuse to march against us, we shall seek you and pursue you. . . . Then we shall see whose favor heaven will declare, and who shall be exalted by victory, and who abased by a shameful defeat."

Like two children daring each other to cross a line, the Thunderbolt and the Earthshaker squared off and prepared for war. Tamerlane, who had defeated Husayn and Toktamish, was now to meet the last of his life's three greatest opponents.

The Turk was busy with the siege of Constantinople when Tamerlane invaded Asia Minor and attacked the walled city of Sivas in August 1400. (It was here that Tamerlane tricked the garrison into opening its gates by promising no blood would be shed and then buried its 4,000 Armenian Christians alive.) Tamerlane followed his conquest of Sivas by overcoming most of Bayazid's border fortresses. Instead of continuing his advances into Bayazid's kingdom, however, Tamerlane spent the next two years putting down revolts in Iraq and Syria. In June 1402 he returned to the Ottoman Empire, determined to dispose of his Turkish enemy once and for all.

The decisive battle was fought at Angora (Ankara, present capital of Turkey) on July 28, 1402. Baya-

This prayer rug, made in Asia Minor during Tamerlane's time, is probably much like the one used by the Mongol warrior for his devotions. A devout Muslim, Tamerlane prostrated himself before every battle to ask Allah for help in defeating his foes.

zid's army, estimated at a quarter of a million men, included Turks, Greeks, and Serbians, the latter "so covered with steel that only their eyes could be seen." The blood-red banners of the janissaries — celebrated warriors recruited from among Christian slaves, whose ferocity was dreaded from the Danube to Egypt — waved above the troops as the sultan's army made its ponderous way toward the waiting Mongol horde.

Tamerlane's army was about the same size as Bayazid's, but the Tartars had the advantage of much larger cavalry units. Furthermore, they were rested, while the Turkish troops arrived exhausted and thirsty after a long forced march to Angora. Finally, Tamerlane's confident men marched against the enemy behind the superweapon of the day — an awesome row of the huge war elephants Tamerlane had captured in India.

The Turks fought heroically, but their infantry skills were no match for the formidable riding abilities of the Tartars. From the backs of the mighty elephants, glittering with steel armor, Tamerlane's men poured streams of liquid fire on the Turks. The sounds of the immense battle roared across the plains northeast of Angora from early morning until nightfall. Through it all, Bayazid fought with his men, wielding his battle-ax as boldly as any of the janissaries around him. When his horse fell at last, it took three Tartars to bind the fierce bearded Turk and carry him to Tamerlane.

The victor received the vanquished courteously. Many legends sprang up about what happened next. Tamerlane had often called Bayazid "the Turk with no sense" and accused him of lacking the vision to understand that he could never defeat the Tartars. Now, some say, Tamerlane smiled at his captive; asked why, he answered, "I smile that God should have given the dominion of the world to a blind man like you and a lame man like me."

At the customary victory banquet that followed the Angora battle, Bayazid was clothed in rich robes, given his jeweled turban and gold mace of office, and served the finest food and wine. The proud sultan, according to some reports, sat rigid and silent

The great city of Konya, once part of the Ottoman Empire, became an independent kingdom after Tamerlane defeated the Ottoman Turks in 1402. To prevent the empire's immediate revival, Tamerlane divided it into small realms, each ruled by a competing prince.

through the feast, without taking a morsel of food. When his wives appeared, stripped like the other women, to serve the Tartar nobles, Bayazid could stand no more and rose, his head bowed, to leave the hall.

After the sultan tried to escape from his tent, he was confined in a barred vehicle on Tamerlane's marches. This circumstance gave rise to a story that the Tartar chief kept his captive in a cage like an animal. It was by this tale that Tamerlane was to become best known in Europe. English playwright Christopher Marlowe used it as the climax of his play about the Mongol's cruelty and ambition, *Tamburlaine the Great*, written 185 years later.

Since Tamerlane expected to receive a huge ransom for Bayazid, it is extremely unlikely that he would have so mistreated his prisoner. It is one of the ironies of history that after all the real atrocities Tamerlane committed, he became most notorious for a crime of which he was probably innocent.

Whatever the circumstances of his imprisonment, Bayazid grew sick in the spring of 1403. Tamerlane sent his own doctor to treat him, but the sultan died in March. Marlowe said the humiliated ruler bashed his own brains out on the bars of his cage; more reliable sources attribute his death to apoplexy or asthma. Tamerlane sent Bayazid's body, with a magnificent honor guard, to the Anatolian capital for burial.

In a series of subsequent campaigns, Tamerlane captured the Ottoman Empire, but he had no interest in ruling it. He divided the once mighty kingdom among a group of independent princes, thus assuring that it would rise no more as a threat during his own lifetime.

Tamerlane's campaign against Bayazid was his last great fight. It is another of the ironies of his life that by defeating Bayazid, the devoutly Muslim Tartar performed a great service to Christianity. Before his war against the Turks, Constantinople had been on the verge of falling to Bayazid and his Muslim army. Tamerlane's capture of the Ottoman Empire delayed the Muslim conquest of Christian Constantinople by half a century.

THE METROPOLITAN MUSEUM OF ART, BEQUEST OF GEORGE C. STONE, 1936

Dressed for war, the troops of Bayazid, sultan of the Ottoman Empire, were a fearsome sight. Their heads were protected by pointed iron helmets, their faces covered by a thick veil of iron mesh.

Two years passed before Tamerlane returned to Samarkand — time spent, as usual, in fierce battle. He attacked Smyrna (now Izmir), a Christian stronghold on the Turkish coast, in late 1402. Bayazid had unsuccessfully besieged Smyrna for seven years, but Tamerlane subdued the walled fortress city in two weeks.

He used siege machines — huge wheeled structures that were rolled up to the walls, allowing the invaders to mount ladders and enter the fort. After overrunning the city, Tamerlane's men beheaded its Christian defenders. When Christian-manned ships appeared, Tamerlane ordered his troops to bombard them with the enemy heads. The ships fled, and Smyrna belonged to Tamerlane.

This was an important victory, because it allowed Tamerlane to label his battles in Turkey as a "holy war" — one fought for the Muslim cause — and helped erase the stigma of his conquest of the Muslim Ottoman Turks.

Tamerlane's satisfaction over his success at Smyrna was soon displaced by grief: the following spring, still en route to Transoxiana, he received word that Muhammad-Sultan, his favorite grandson and chosen successor, was dangerously ill. Tamerlane rushed to the camp of the young man, who had been on his way to join his grandfather. Nothing could be done to save Muhammad-Sultan, however, and he died a few weeks later.

Ordering a huge and solemn funeral service, the aging Tartar chief sent for his family. When Muhammad-Sultan's three young sons arrived, Tamerlane's tough, leathery face, for the first time in anyone's memory, was streaked with tears.

Tamerlane arrived in Transoxiana in 1404. Now 67 years old, he was nearly blind. His crippled right leg had worsened, and he could walk or ride only with pain and difficulty. His appetite for war, however, was undiminished; perhaps it grew keener as he saw his time running out. The celebration at his return was unrestrained, and for a few days he permitted himself to relax and enjoy it. Then his thoughts once more turned to conquest.

Tamerlane wanted a new challenge. He was al-

When the army of Bayazid the Thunderbolt met that of Tamerlane the Earthshaker in 1402, the men of both sides were heavily armored. The Turks' battle dress included a breastplate made of iron bands and a skirt of linked iron strips.

ready supreme master of central Asia and Asia Minor, and he considered Europe's poor and feeble nations beneath his notice. The only goal worthy of his attention was the richest of the world's great empires: China. Conquered in 1259 by Genghis Khan's grandson Kublai, China had been a Mongol possession for barely a century before a native chief had rebelled, driving the last of the khan's descendants from the throne in Peking in the 1360s.

An invasion of China, argued Tamerlane, would be a holy war. It would not only avenge the insult to the Mongol race; it would enable his men to "cleanse their swords of the blood of their fellow Muslims, the Ottomans, by washing them in that of the infidels of China." His soldiers, who had been through so much with the lame chieftain, would follow him anywhere, and the council of amirs was no less loyal to his service. Tamerlane made ready for the 4,000-mile march.

Ignoring the bitter winter weather, the indomitable old warrior set out from Samarkand in late 1404. After a 250-mile ride, he and his men reached the Transoxianian border city of Otrar, where 200,000 soldiers had been assembled to begin the campaign. But here the Earthshaker met an even greater conqueror than himself. A sudden, violent fever seized his now frail body.

Aware that he had little remaining time, Tamerlane named his successor: Pir-Muhammad, his 29-year-old grandson. Pir-Muhammad was the son of Jahangir, the Tartar chief's firstborn son, who had died a quarter of a century earlier. "I order you," said Tamerlane, "to obey him and serve him . . . so that the world will not fall into disorder, and the work of so many years of my life be lost." Then the Earthshaker expressed the hope that "God will pardon my sins, which are many. . . ."

A witness — clearly no admirer of Tamerlane — described the death scene with vindictive relish: "Neither his wealth nor his children availed him ought, and he began to vomit blood and bite his hands with grief. . . . He coughed like a camel that is strangled, his color was nigh quenched, and his cheeks foamed like a camel dragged backwards. . . . At last he was carried to the cursing and punishment of God, remaining in torment and God's infernal punishment."

Tamerlane's court historian was kinder. The Lord of the Fortunate Conjunction, he reported, was called by the angel of Allah, who said, "O hopeful spirit, return to your lord with resignation. We are of God, and we return to him." Then, said the chronicler, Tamerlane entered Paradise. It was the night of February 18, 1405.

When Tamerlane died, the expedition to China

After a 53-day siege in 1453, Turkish troops overrun Constantinople, the center of Eastern Christianity. Tamerlane's crushing defeat of the Ottoman Turks in 1402 delayed the Muslim conquest of the pivotal Mediterranean port city (now Istanbul, Turkey) for half a century.

Genghis Khan's grandson Kublai Khan, who ruled China from 1259 until 1294, uses a falcon to hunt deer. A brilliant military leader, Kublai was also a patron of art and literature. The fall of his dynasty in the 1360s left China open to conquest, a situation Tamerlane found hard to resist.

was abandoned. Above all things, the Tartar leader had wished that "the work of so many years" of his life be made safe, but this was not to be. Tamerlane's empire had owed its existence to the irresistible force of his own personality. Without him, it soon began to disintegrate. He had named Pir-Muhammad as overall ruler, but he had also parceled out huge sections of his empire to his two remaining sons, Miran-Shah and Shah-Rukh, and to many of his grandsons. The Tartar heirs began to quarrel and fight for power immediately.

Pir-Muhammad was in Afghanistan at the time of his grandfather's death. Closer to the seat of power was Miran-Shah's son Khalil, who seized the throne at once. A year later, Pir-Muhammad was assassinated and Khalil was overthrown by his own nobles, who proclaimed Tamerlane's youngest son, Shah-Rukh, as their leader.

Shah-Rukh proved to be an able and wise ruler. Far less warlike than Tamerlane, he was both a competent military man and a patron of the arts. Like his grandfather, he was a dedicated builder. Historians have called Shah-Rukh's reign, which lasted from 1407 until 1447, "the golden age of Persian literature and art."

Shah-Rukh, however, ruled only part of Tamerlane's empire — Transoxiana itself and a section of western Persia. When he died, his kingdom, in the

THE BETTMANN ARCHIVE

Janissaries (whose name meant "new soldiers" in Turkish) were members of an elite unit in the armies of the Ottoman Turks. Recruited from among Christian captives, they were formidable fighters, feared and respected by Christians and Muslims alike.

Builder as well as destroyer, Tamerlane left an enduring mark on the old city of Samarkand. Many of the buildings he constructed, now carefully preserved and restored by the Soviet government, look much as they did when they were new, more than five centuries ago.

words of historian Edward Gibbon, "was again involved in darkness and blood." The rest of the old Tartar chief's domains, scenes of ongoing battles for power, gradually fell to outside invaders. Less than a century after Tamerlane's death, his empire had vanished, and his dynasty was extinguished.

Tamerlane was unquestionably the most remarkable and contradictory man of his time. He was worshiped by his people and respected by European monarchs, but his name became a byword for cruelty and unquenchable, mad ambition. Songs about his exploits are still sung in Asia, songs of yearning for the time when such giants strode the earth.

His goal was the reconstruction and enlargement of Genghis Khan's empire, but he never really tried to create a unified nation. Conquest was often an end in itself for the Earthshaker. Historian Bertold Spuler, in his book *Les Mongoles dans l'Histoire*, dismisses Tamerlane as having had "no precise objective. . . . His activity had no significance in the evolution and the progress of civilization in Asia, and many of his enterprises can only be characterized as brigandage and pillage."

Tamerlane was indeed a brigand and a killer on an unprecedented scale — the number of lives he is estimated to have taken is 18 million — but he was also a builder. The buildings he constructed to glorify his bloody achievements remain the finest examples of their style of architecture. His reign, and that of his son, produced an extraordinary flowering of art. Painting, writing, architecture, calligraphy, and many other arts flourished in what is called the Timurid period.

More important, this "scourge of God," as Marlowe called him, was responsible for a return to order in a time of anarchy. He reestablished the "Mongolian Peace" that his predecessor Genghis Khan had briefly enforced. It was said of Tamerlane that "under his prosperous monarchy a child, fearless and unhurt, might carry a purse of gold from the East to the West."

Tamerlane's great capital, Samarkand, became an important center of trade between China and India to the east, Europe and Africa to the west.

Rising above a peaceful Samarkand park, a massive blue dome shelters the remains of the "Conqueror of the World." Tamerlane's mighty empire had rested on his own shoulders; within a century of his death in 1405, it had fallen to pieces.

Through Samarkand passed silk and precious stones from China, spices from India, furs from northern Russia. A Spanish ambassador to Tamerlane's court noted that a caravan from China passing through Samarkand included 800 camels, each loaded with precious cargo. Along with all these riches, inevitably, came an exchange of ideas and art, technology and skills. And thus, in blood and fire and death, civilization makes its painful progress through the ages.

Further Reading

Barthold, Vasili. *Four Studies in the History of Central Asia.* London: Luzac & Co., 1956–62.

Gonzales de Clavijo, Ruy. *Embassy to Tamerlane.* New York: Harper & Brothers, 1928.

Grousset, René. *The Empire of the Steppes.* New Brunswick, NJ: Rutgers University Press, 1970.

Hambly, Gavin, ed. *Central Asia.* New York: Delacorte Press, 1969.

Hookham, Hilda. *Tamburlaine the Conqueror.* London: Hodder and Stoughton, 1962.

Ibn-Arabshah, Achmed. *Tamerlane, or Timur the Great.* London: Luzac & Co., 1936.

Lamb, Harold. *Tamerlane, The Earth Shaker.* Garden City, NY: Garden City Publishing Co., 1929.

Prawdin, Michael. *The Mongol Empire: Its Rise and Legacy.* London: George Allen & Unwin, 1961.

Sykes, Sir Percy. *A History of Persia.* London: Macmillan & Co., 1930.

Vernadsky, George. *The Mongols and Russia.* New Haven: Yale University Press, 1953.

Chronology

April 9, 1336	Born Timur in Transoxiana (part of the present-day Soviet Union), the son of a minor noble in the nomadic Barlas clan
1360	Tughlugh-Timur, a Jat khan, conquers Transoxiana; Tamerlane enters his service and is named prince of Samarkand
	Tamerlane stages an unsuccessful rebellion against Tughlugh and flees into the desert
1362	Tamerlane and his brother-in-law Husayn lead a band of mercenary warriors
1363	Tughlugh dies; Tamerlane and Husayn drive the Jats out of Transoxiana
1365	Tughlugh's son, Ilyas, attacks Transoxiana, defeating Tamerlane and Husayn at the "Battle of the Mire"
	The citizens of Samarkand successfully resist Ilyas's troops
1366	Tamerlane and Husayn disband Samarkand's civilian government; Husayn becomes amir, Tamerlane his second-in-command
1366–69	Tamerlane and Husayn end their alliance and fight sporadically
1370	Tamerlane defeats Husayn at Balkh; Husayn is killed
	Becomes great lord of Transoxiana
1375	Tamerlane's favorite son, Jahangir, dies
1376–78	Supports Toktamish's battle against the khan of the White Horde
1378	Toktamish becomes khan of the White Horde
1380	Tamerlane begins a series of campaigns in Persia and conquers Herat, in present-day Afghanistan
	Toktamish defeats the khan of the Golden Horde and becomes the leader of the united White and Golden Hordes
1387–88	Toktamish invades Transoxiana; is finally driven out by Tamerlane's troops
1391	Tamerlane defeats Toktamish at the Battle of Kunduzcha
1393	Successfully attacks the Persian city of Shiraz and the kingdom of Iraq
	Death of Tamerlane's son Omar-Sheik
1398	Invades and conquers much of India
July 28, 1402	Tamerlane defeats the Ottoman Turks at the Battle of Angora and takes Sultan Bayazid captive
1403	Tamerlane's heir-apparent, his grandson Muhammad-Sultan, dies
1404	Mounts an expedition to conquer China
Feb. 18, 1405	Dies of a fever

Index

Dennis Wepman has a graduate degree in linguistics from Columbia University and has written widely on sociology, linguistics, popular culture, and American folklore. He now teaches English at City University of New York, Queens College. He is the author of *Alexander the Great, Simón Bolívar, Hernán Cortés, Adolf Hitler, Benito Juárez,* and *Jomo Kenyatta* in the Chelsea House series WORLD LEADERS   PAST & PRESENT.

Arthur M. Schlesinger, jr., taught history at Harvard for many years and is currently Albert Schweitzer Professor of the Humanities at City University of New York. He is the author of numerous highly praised works in American history and has twice been awarded the Pulitzer Prize. He served in the White House as special assistant to Presidents Kennedy and Johnson.